Little White Whys

A Woman's Guide through the Lies Men Tell and Why

I. MAJOR, MD

iUniverse, Inc.
New York   Bloomington

Little White Whys
A Woman's Guide through the Lies Men Tell and Why

The views expressed in this work are solely those of the author
and do not necessarily reflect the views of the publisher, and the
publisher hereby disclaims any responsibility for them.

iUniverse books may be ordered through booksellers or by contacting:

iUniverse
1663 Liberty Drive
Bloomington, IN 47403
www.iuniverse.com
1-800-Authors (1-800-288-4677)

Because of the dynamic nature of the Internet, any Web addresses or
links contained in this book may have changed since publication and
may no longer be valid. The views expressed in this work are solely those
of the author and do not necessarily reflect the views of the publisher,
and the publisher hereby disclaims any responsibility for them.

ISBN: 978-0-595-53080-9 (pbk)
ISBN: 978-0-595-51818-0 (cloth)
ISBN: 978-0-595-63136-0 (ebk)

Library of Congress Control Number: 2009933829

Printed in the United States of America

iUniverse rev. date: 10/20/2009

Contents

Foreword

This is a daring debut. Dr. Major, a board-certified psychiatrist, has helped many people grapple with heartbreak and mental exhaustion with regard to relationships. He believes that, by navigating the dating world fully equipped, the odds will be in your favor.

While Dr. Major functions daily as a hard-nosed, serious psychiatrist, he is also a realist, maybe a little bit dark, who knows just enough about the dating world to offer us a creative, yet honest, account about what really takes place in the minds of men. In addition, he offers the truth about why men lie.

It is evident by the increasing divorce statistics and the barrage of dating tools (such as Match.com, eHarmony, and It's Just Lunch) that many people need a little more assistance in this area. This book comes at just the right time, as we, single people interested in dating, are progressing to a technological approach to dating. Technology has made a personal process somewhat impersonal and has perhaps created a great recipe for continued deceit and manipulation. In addition, with the rise in online dating, there is also a rise in "first dates"; hence, we need a no-nonsense guide to help lead the way. *Little White Whys* is just the guide.

Dr. Major begins the book discussing first dates and intentions. He provides a critical account of what women should focus on, what *not* to fall for, and the right questions to ask. Each chapter provides a scenario and the common mistakes women make in deciphering lies and male intentions. Dr. Major has included "pop quizzes," which are realistic and functional. Most importantly, the quizzes allow for an analysis of the dating world.

Dr. Major also lists and explains many common lies told by men to women. This book captures the essence of the difficulties and challenges that plague the dating arena. You will feel empowered and uplifted as you begin to understand the male psyche and find more satisfaction and success in your dating life.

—Kimberly Brown, PhD, psychologist

Introduction

"Hi, I'm Dr. Major. It's nice to meet you. Come in, have a seat, and tell me a little bit about what's been going on." That's the way I usually start when I meet a new patient in my psychiatric practice. What follows next is often a life story filled with twists and turns, lost hope, and broken trust in a relationship. After five years of college, four years of medical school, three years of a psychiatric residency, two years of a specialty fellowship in child and adolescent psychiatry, and a board certification in the field of psychiatry, one would think I'd be prepared. Every patient who comes to see me deserves my best, and that's exactly what I try to give them. I graduated from medical school in 2000 and have been in solo practice since 2005. In that time, I've treated thousands of patients and families. I specialize in child psychiatry but have always had a special interest in couples. The years of practice have definitely added polish to my approach, but beneath that, it still hurts to see another person in pain. Part of what my patients like about me is that I'm not afraid to show them that. I don't always promise success, but I always promise to try. That's hope. Sometimes that's all we need to get through the tough times.

I'd have to say that the overwhelming majority of the time when people, both patients and friends, come to me with feelings of depression or anxiety, these feelings stem from issues with relationships. Relationships get tough when expectations aren't met. Relationships get tough when promises aren't kept.

Relationships get tough when trust gets broken. The fact that we cannot control another person in a relationship is, all at once, exciting, scary, and frustrating. What we can do is try to understand the other person. We can try to see the other person very clearly for who he or she really is.

In this book, I am going to take a journey through every phase of a relationship and try to understand the exact reasons why things turn out the way they turn out. Ray Charles has an "oldie but goodie" called "Understanding." In that song, he simply and plainly explains that understanding is the best thing in the world between a boy and a girl. Very basic, but oh so true. What I hope you get from this book is a better understanding of why men say and do some of the seemingly odd things we say and do.

It is my sincere hope that this book can serve as a guide for women who are trying to navigate through the sea of choices when it comes to meeting, getting to know, dating, falling in love with, and committing to that special someone. This is a precise reference book of men's lies. And this book also serves as a very basic reminder that, if things appear one way but feel another way in your relationship, then he may be lying to you. Ladies, what I will attempt to do is give you an intimate tour of the workings of the male mind. There will be secrets revealed and truths uncovered, and parts of this book will be painful to read—exquisitely so, because at some point along this road, I'm going to ask you to look at the role each of you play in your relationships. Sometimes the truth can be brazen and very tough to hear, because not only are we hearing the truth about that other person, but also we're seeing some truth about ourselves.

Here are three simple truths when it comes to dating men:
1. *Believe half of what we say and all of what we do.* That's a pretty safe first rule to what we will be discussing here, which are relationships from the male point of view.

What I'm going to give you here is something that probably precious few men have ever given you before … the truth. It's up to you, what you do with it. Dating is such a simple concept. We are the ones who make it hard. It should be easy—or at least that's what I tell people. Don't just ask questions; ask the *right* questions. Listen to the answers, but believe what we show you. Do not, I repeat, do not let your own issues confuse you. By "issues," I mean those wants and needs and insecurities that we all share, which lead us to act how we act and do what we do. Ladies, you cannot allow the emotion connected with what you want to cloud or confuse the issue of what is. You simply must find a way to allow yourself the objectivity to see your relationships clearly. It is with this same objectivity that most, if not all, males look upon their relationships as well.

2. *Guys only want one thing—sex.* I know it's an old cliché, but things usually become old clichés for a reason, which is that they are true. Now, the caveat here is, what exactly are guys willing to do and say and put up with or endure, to get sex?

3. *Everything you need to know about us, we told you during our first three conversations.* Frightening but true, ladies. Think back for a moment, pretend you're a Jedi knight (as most men often do), and "search your feelings" … you'll find it to be true.

I'll tell you what this book is about by telling you what it's not. It is not a how-to book about dating. Instead, this is simply a tool to help you as a woman gain some understanding into why we as men think the things we think, do the things we do, and consequently have had some of the outcomes we all have had. For guys, this book can be a tool or barometer to see if anything in this book reminds you of yourselves and if so, why? My intent is for ladies to be able to use this book as a handy dandy guide to the lies men may be telling them in the various stages of their relationships.

What I will attempt to do is take you through each phase of a relationship and offer different scenarios, so you may have a better grasp of the possibilities of what may and may not happen and why. Ladies, prepare; this will be brutally honest and may "sting a little" … (sorry, it's the MD in me). Guys, I'm sorry, but, yes, I will tell exactly what we think and feel (yes, we feel too), and I will say the things that most of us are simply too terrified to utter if a woman is within fifty feet of us. At times, the tone of this book will be condescending, sophomoric, stupefying, moronic, immature, and downright childlike. Ladies, when was the last time you were in a relationship with a man who didn't possess firm command of at least one, if not all, of these traits? Ah yes, the art here is truly imitating life. Ladies, if I offend you, I do apologize beforehand. If I oversimplify things at times, again, sorry.

The goal here is for you to be able to spend your time in meaningful, fulfilling, loving, and, yes, lasting relationships. That can only begin with truth. Disappointment occurs when what you wanted or expected to happen did not happen. If you start with the truth, then you will know exactly what to expect, and your chances of being disappointed in relationships will be drastically reduced.

My more suspicious readers may now be asking this: "Okay, Dr. Truth, if you're a guy on the dating scene, why would you write a book like this, telling all of you and your boys' secrets?"

Good question. The truth is because it's only fair. The truth is because I have five sisters and a mother whom I love fiercely and would give anything and everything not to see them hurt. The truth is that all of you ladies reading this book are someone's daughter, sister, or mother—and so I don't want to see you being continuously hurt either. I am certified by the American Board of Psychiatry and Neurology to treat adults with all forms of mental illness. I have received specialty training to be able to treat both children and adolescents. As a result, I usually end up treating the whole family. This allows me a unique perspective on what effect healthy relationships have on all family members and just what effect not-so-healthy relationships have as well. The truth is that every day, I'm confronted with patients at the end of their proverbial ropes of life and, more often than not, at the heart of their exasperation is a failed relationship.

The facts are clear. In 2002, the divorce rate in the United States was 52 percent. Today, that number has declined to 36 percent.[1] That is to say, roughly four out of every ten marriages ends in divorce. Of the couples who stay married, only 38 percent describe themselves as "happily married."[2] Here's another fact: loss and separation are the most common causes of sadness in children.[3] There are few things more devastating to a child than the loss or perceived loss of a parent. There are few things more heart wrenching to this psychiatrist than the tears in the eyes of some of those very sad, clinically depressed children. So, in a way, I'm backtracking. In order to help prevent some of the pathology I see in my patients, I will make an effort to help you avoid one of the most traumatic things that can occur in a person's life: divorce. Sometimes it's hard to see the widespread effects of choices we make as adults. Oftentimes, I see children who weren't placed very high on the decision-making tree. Divorce can have a wide range of effects on children. Children of divorce can display behavioral changes, academic problems, low self-esteem, and difficulty getting along with siblings, peers, and parents. Adolescents from a divorced home are more likely to engage in delinquent activities, to get involved in early sexual activity, and experiment with illicit drugs.[4] The point is that relationship issues don't just affect the two people in that relationship. They affect everyone.

I have treated thousands of patients in my psychiatric practice. The majority of their diagnoses have been some form of depression or anxiety. If there is a clear cause, most of the time, it all goes back to a relationship with a significant other, past or present, that somehow took a wrong turn. This book is an attempt at preventative medicine. While it's an honor and a privilege for me to treat patients in a psychiatric setting, the hope here is to help you all with one of the most important parts of your lives now, so you may be able to avoid seeing me or another psychiatrist once things have unraveled and ended poorly.

So I think it's just time to get real and get really honest about what exactly it is we're all doing here, hoping for clarity of purpose and intent, so that we may all be better prepared when that moment, that meeting, that special person comes into our lives. The train ride to regret is very long and very bumpy. You don't want to have to look back on these situations and think about what you wished you should have, would have, and could have said or done.

The first love letter I ever wrote read something like this:
Hi, Vanessa,
I like you.
Do you like me?
Check yes or no.

Short, simple, straight to the point. What it lacked in imagery, it surely made up for in sense of purpose. Wow, that seems like a lifetime ago—or at least it does to me. Were relationships ever really that simple? For some of us, things surely have gotten complicated, it seems. For others still, things always were difficult and still are. As we grow, we all have our share of trials and tribulations, disappointments and triumphs, and life events that have helped shape our behavior. We are the sum total of our life experiences. It's what we choose to do with these experiences that makes our lives interesting. Choice is an interesting word. Let's crack that trusty Webster's dictionary and get a definition:

choice:

noun

1: the act of choosing: selection <finding it hard to make a *choice*>

2: power of choosing: option <you have no *choice*>

3 **a:** the best part: cream **b:** a person or thing chosen <she was their first *choice*>

4: a number and variety to choose among <a plan with a wide *choice* of options>

5: care in selecting

6: a grade of meat between prime and good[5]

I like number 2 and number 5: the power of choosing and care in selecting. When someone comes to my psychiatric practice for relationship advice, the first thing I point out to the patient is that his or her current relationship is the way it is because of a series of choices that individual made at some point in that relationship—some choices were good and a lot were probably bad. This is, at the same time, both an empowering and a frightening concept. Empowering, because if we have choices, that means we can always change things. Terrifying, because if it is up to us to make these choices, we begin to wonder if we are really prepared and qualified to do a good job with the choices. Well, sure you are. There are millions of healthy relationships out there that are proof positive that it can be done. So what's their secret? At the risk of oversimplifying, I would say that, at some point in their lives, the people in the relationships each undertook some serious self-reflection time or gained a firm knowledge of themselves. They chose to then be transparent with others whom they chose to date. They chose what things they did and did not want in a relationship, and then together set about a way to honestly build a relationship based on just that—honesty. What are the ingredients for a healthy relationship? One source sites seven key ingredients:

1. Mutual respect
2. Trust

3. Honesty
4. Support
5. Fairness/equality
6. Separate identities
7. Good communication[6]

Here, we're going to focus primarily on the honesty, but all the ingredients eventually come into play. After reading this book, you, too, will be better equipped to quickly and concisely make good choice after good choice in an effort to help build and maintain healthy relationships.

I'm going to be using a lot of analogies—a lot of "guy-specific" analogies. For instance, tools. There has long been a connection between men and their tools. We like them. We need a lot of them, the more the better, and we also need large, isolated, secluded spaces to put them in, so we can find them quickly if and when they are needed. "The right tool for the right job," I always say. And we remember to put those tools away when we're done with them—usually. If not, someone could get hurt! Stepping on a rake or hammer or accidentally sitting on a screwdriver could be painful! Well, for guys, the truth is just that—a tool. We pull it out and use it when we need it but then tuck it away neatly after it is no longer needed. Unfortunately, we also forget to put the truth completely away sometimes. We clumsily leave it lying about in our cars, our wallets, our cell phone call logs, our bedrooms, etc. And more times than not, the lady or ladies in our life eventually stumble upon it and *wham-o*—somebody gets hurt!

Someone much smarter than I once said, "Women are attracted to the men they fall in love with; men fall in love with the women they are attracted to." If you can understand the meaning behind that, then we can take a deeper look into the "whys" of male dating behavior.

THE MEETING

Okay, here's where it all begins: the meeting. Ladies, please understand that most guys are self-proclaimed masters of the "chance meeting." It's romantic and innocent, and we know you'll be telling the story to every female friend you have who's within earshot. The only question is how well rehearsed the meeting will be. Some of us pride ourselves (myself included) on the amount of polish we can display at this point—and rightfully so, because a lot is riding on this moment. Guys know and firmly believe that you can and will decide within the first five minutes of meeting us whether or not we will ever get to see you naked. It's true. You know it, we know it, and everything we do from this point on will all be heading toward one of three directions: the naked zone, the friend zone, or the boyfriend developmental league.

The naked zone—well it's obvious—you will be sleeping with the guy at some point, and it's just a matter of when and how often. The friend zone (sadly, guys) is where there is absolutely no hope of advancement or promotion in the relationship. For some of us guys, this zone is sheer misery (especially if we're still harboring ideas of becoming romantic with you). Here is the area where guys get way too much information about you ladies. You will bludgeon us with the gory details of damn near every relationship you have ever had and the things you've tried sexually (which is particularly painful for us guys to hear, by the way). We get the unabridged version of the life and times of all of the current and remarkable past female friends you have ever had, and then you tie all that up with a neat little "I'm so glad we're friends, so I can talk to you about this stuff" bow. Yes, ladies, this zone can be excruciating and quite challenging even for the more effeminate and gay or bi-curious of us gents.

So why would we do it? Why would we allow ourselves to, week in and week out, hear about all the shit we will probably never get to do to (excuse me) with you? It's quite simple really. In the male mind, egocentric place that it is, we never truly believe that we're out of the game. We think we always have a shot at the naked zone. Sad but true, ladies. The second reason is this (and doesn't involve you as much): at some point, we plan to sleep with one (or more) of your friends (see above). Yes, ladies, it's true, and it should be obvious. Hell, you are practically begging us to do it. You might as well just give us a key to their bedroom doors and their precious little hearts because we plan on seizing both. They are a predetermined group of women whom we will meet, whom you've told us everything about, every flaw and every weakness, and they already love us because we are "so sweet" to just want to be your friend and not get in your pants. For us guys, it's a slam dunk; it's a no-brainer (actually most of the things we do and say require surprisingly little brains ... but no matter). Okay, so you might ask "How do we keep you from trying to sleep with our friends?" It's quite simple. Stop telling us about them. Period. Here's how the male mind works at this moment: you tell us about a place, and we want to go there. The first time I heard about Disney World, I wanted to go there. The first time I heard about the wild parties in Miami, I wanted to go there. You can't tell us about a strange and exotic land and expect us as men not to want to go there and explore it and eventually conquer it … it's who we are … it's what we do … sorry. There, I said it … sorry, guys.

And now that brings us to the developmental league, doesn't it? A little place women like to call "the back burner," where the guys have "potential" but need to work on one or two key elements to the woman's accommodation. What might that be? Hell, it could be anything: weight, hygiene, employment, geographical location … the list can be as long as my … err … arm. But guys, don't despair, because if you pay attention to the regularly scheduled conversations she will allow you in this league, she (as any good coach) will tell you exactly what elements of your game you need to work on. Just listen. We know you're looking for trainability at this point, ladies, and so what we will do is give you regular updates on our progress (even if we're not making any) … damn those lies men tell. We'll say stuff like "oh yeah, I joined a new gym" (not the one you go to, by the way), or "I'm taking a new class in blah blah blah," or "I'm thinking about getting a new car," or "I'm thinking about getting a new place," or "I'm thinking about getting a new job." Basically, ladies, we are "thinking" about doing anything new that will give you a new mental picture of us and help us get those new panties … yours!

Now that we all know the places that this meeting may go, let's get into the actual meeting itself. What are we thinking? Well, I assure you, it's not as remotely romantic as what you're gonna come up with. It's actually quite practical and systematic for us. What I've learned as a psychiatrist is this: from the moment we meet someone, we immediately begin to try to categorize him or her. It's a subconscious thing. Our minds are constantly trying to make sense of the world around us; it never stops. The way we do that is by putting everything in its place. We take what is unknown and try to fit it into a known space, so we can better understand it. So for guys, our first category for a woman is appearance or looks. It's the first thing we notice. Simply put—*is she hot or not?* And if so, exactly how hot? Guys amuse themselves with the cute little names we use to grade you ladies. (It's degrading, I know). There's *smokin' hot, hot, really cute,* and *just okay.* The names may vary from guy to guy or group to group, but the categories remain the same.

Smokin' hot is self-evident. It means that physically, you are "Lex Luger," the total package (sorry, ladies, he was an old-school wrestler, and all guys have watched it, so look into it). Smokin' hot means your face is gorgeous, breasts are pert and perky, perfect ass is incredible, legs go on and on and on like an Erykah Badu song, and the feet and toes are too cute for words. Upon first seeing this spectacle, the typical guy will actually need to take a minute and a few long stares to gather himself and adjust his approach. Now, I'm gonna let you in on a well-kept secret: most smokin' hot women rarely get approached. While I can't say it is the "fear of God" that causes guys not to approach these women, I would imagine it's pretty close. Simply put, we are intimidated. I know it's cliché, and pretty girls say that all the time, but in this case, it's actually true. For a guy, there is no more distasteful an idea than the thought of getting totally turned down by a smokin' hot woman. The devastation would be great and measurable, and we would continue to replay the horrific scene in our minds for months to come. Honestly, it should have been a task on that television show *Fear Factor.* Men: approach a beautiful stranger and attempt to charm her in hopes of obtaining her contact information. A lot of guys would leave that episode broke and pissed! For many of us, fear is definitely a factor here.

So how do we prevent that fear? It's easy; we avoid direct contact with you ... smokin' hot girl. You're kinda like a mythical creature—you know, like unicorns and dragons and such. Best appreciated from afar so as not to ruin the legend. I mean, I love watching movies about dragons, but what would I really do with one in real life? I tell women in my practice all the time that being beautiful is practically a handicap. It's ironic when you think about it. Unfortunately, this culture has such high regard for all things beautiful that we automatically assign certain attributes to beautiful people and make all sorts of assumptions about them. "Look at her … she looks so … happy. What problems could she possible have with her cute little self? She probably goes out on a date with a different guy every night." And so on and so forth. We even assume that most attractive people are successful and wealthy … you know it's true. So the beautiful woman is handicapped in dating, because most guys will never be able to see past her appearance. Guys will typically only be able to relate to her on a physical level, which is unfortunate, because the true woman on the inside will never be seen, and we all end up missing out on what is typically a pretty cool person. It's not fair, I know, and it's our hang up … I know that too.

What I tell people is that beautiful people look at themselves in the mirror every day, so the way they look isn't that big of a deal to them. It's just a part of who they are—regular, normal people. I get very basic here and say that beautiful women are actually just like the rest of us; they sleep when they are tired, eat (sometimes) when they are hungry, cry when they are sad, and call me when they are horny … ahhh … only in a perfect world. Sorry. Okay, seriously, there are basically two types of men who will approach the stunningly beautiful woman. Either the total loser or the uberarrogant. The loser will approach because he has no remaining ego to be destroyed. He is under no delusions about the zilch he has to offer and has nothing to lose by venturing an introduction. And if and when he is turned away, it's no great surprise to him; he figured it was coming at some point. Then there is the super successful, super arrogant (sometimes equally attractive) guy whose narcissistic ego is so massive that he is impervious to rejection—on the surface. "Clearly you don't know what you're missing." I know a few of you ladies have heard that before.

In either case, ladies, just move on. It's not worth the time and effort (or cost of dinner that you're gonna buy if you pick the loser). Smokin' hot ladies, here's what you have to do to meet a regular guy. You have to go above and beyond the call, to let us know you're actually approachable and nice. You're gonna have to smile a little more, give off some "approach me" body language, make some direct eye contact, and maybe, just maybe, you're gonna have to say "hi" first … it's a shocker, I know, but trust me; there is no better icebreaker than just saying hello, and any guy who's worth getting to know will respond in kind.

That brings us to you, hot girl. You present a different kind of conundrum for guys. We have to decide what exactly we want to do with you. Which largely depends on if we are actually single or not at the time we meet you. Maybe we're looking to upgrade our current lady to "hot girl 4.0." Maybe we simply want to have a sexual relationship with you. Maybe we want to put you on the "back burner." We will almost immediately begin to turn our conversation toward that end, and if you pay close attention, you will be able to tell exactly where it is we're trying to take you.

If we're single and really into you, it will progress as you would expect it would, to phone calls, pertinent questions about you, dinner, dates, and general enjoyment from being in your presence. Ladies, remember this: normal things are normal, and the truth makes sense. When you begin to not understand "where he's coming from," that's a sign that he's trying to take you somewhere you don't want to go or put you in a position that you were not expecting.

If we just want sex, ladies, you will hear key phrases like "I'm just enjoying being single right now," or "I'm really just dating right now, but nobody serious," or "Most women are so possessive," or "I'm not really a talk-on-the-phone kind of person," or "I hate planning stuff; I just like to be spontaneous." You get the picture. We will never make any definite plans with you (especially not on a Saturday because, as we all know, that is the day strictly reserved for significant others), we will never have a phone conversation with you lasting over ten minutes, and you will absolutely not under any circumstances ever meet any member of our families, no matter how long we've known you. Again, don't ignore the obvious signs, ladies. And let me be clear here: if this is not what you want, then do not, I repeat, do not let us continue to sleep with you—period!

There's a peculiar little area of subculture in the realm of "definite interest." A little place called the back burner. The back burner is just that: not a priority. Whatever is on the back burner will continue to simmer nicely for as long as we want until we're ready to take it out of the pan, put it on our plate, and eat you ... err ... it! You, my dear, are our benchwarmers. Not quite talented enough to make the first string or starting lineup but definitely talented enough to not throw away. We know in our hearts that you should have a place on our team, but we're just not sure where and when we're gonna be able to use you in a "game situation." You will provide us with lots of worthwhile workouts in our "practice dates" while we tune up for the real deal with our first-string girls. Brutal, isn't it? I know. Sorry. First rule for the back burner girl is that guys never sleep with the back burner girl (or at least I highly advise against it). That's a no-no. Nakedness here ruins the dynamic and natural progression of what we're trying to do. It clouds the issue, and what we want here is clarity. We'll call when we can, give you an excuse like "I've been so busy with work," or "things are just crazy for me right now." The conversations or occasional lunch or dinner we may have with you, we typically enjoy, and we are genuinely interested in getting to know you. For us guys, our time with you like this is like a series of interviews for the position of "new girlfriend." It's light, fun, no pressure, and a welcome escape from the usual intricacies of a normal relationship.

Pay attention, ladies: this is where you have a chance to really let us get to know and love the real you! Interestingly enough, I've found that relationships that start here and progress to dating from this point typically are more fulfilling and longer lasting. Why? Because you both started with no pretense and no pressure of dating and were able to relax around each other and really get to know each other. There's probably some sage wisdom in doing it this way, but alas, that's not what we typically do, is it?

Now, for the "really cute" or "just okay" woman. Unfortunately, you are going to be dealing with a whole different kind of man animal here. In the male mind, you are immediately classified as (and I'll apologize beforehand for this one) "fuckable" ... ouch! It stings, I know, but bear with me. I'm trying to help you through this and show you how to make your time meaningful. Your challenge, "cute girl," is to not let us put you in that box of "booty calls." You're familiar, you know, with the calls after 9 or 10 PM, the spontaneous "we should do something" conversations that last less than five minutes, and the high probability that not only will you not be spending the night with us, but if you attempt to spend the night, we will also react poorly with rudeness and kick you out. It is what it is. But fear not, cute girl. You have an excellent chance of steering this relationship where you want it. The key is to make us respect you! Do not tolerate late night calls. Do not be overly available to our every whim and fancy. And lastly, do not, under any circumstances, ever, (forever ever?), yes, forever ever sleep with us! Let me repeat that: do not allow yourself to sleep with us! Again, it changes the thrust of the relationship and virtually guarantees you of no chance in hell of ever progressing to a normal relationship with us. Ladies, here you want to get to know us from afar. Let us see exactly how much you value yourself and respect yourself and exactly how much you have your shit together. Trust me; we will notice and will be drawn to you. Ladies, a large part of where this relationship goes from here is up to you. Only, you have to be clear on what you want and stick to the rules—because we surely will.

Pop Quiz:

1. I'm a regular, everyday cute (some days sexy), employed, socially well-adjusted male, and I just happen to be in Barnes and Noble one Saturday afternoon. I have just nestled into a chair to read a grippingly powerful article on "car horsepower and the women that it attracts," when all of a sudden, there arose such a clatter, I sprang to my feet to see what was the matter. Actually, it is more a "click-clack." That oh-so-familiar click-clack of sexy heels worn by pretty women. I peek around the corner and spy with my little eye … her, in all of her glory. *Wow! She's gorgeous! What eyes! What lips! Cute hairstyle. Flirty shirt but not overly done, accentuating what it needs to. Amazing legs! And ass … jeez … didn't know they made denim that could do that now! And yes, sexy heels!* My ears are never wrong. She's standing in the children's books section, but there are no children with her. Her bag is large enough to carry "Mom stuff," but far too stylish to ferry baby wipes and Huggies about. No wedding ring on her finger? Check. Pleasant look on her face? Check. Doesn't appear to be in a rush? Check. Is not currently involved in a conversation on her cell phone? Check. The third-base coach on my shoulder is waving me home! I make my approach and say, "I've always been a fan of *Green Eggs and Ham* myself … what about you?"

What are we thinking ladies? What's our level of interest at this point?

A. *Out of my league!* Because what I didn't notice from afar but see now is that the heels making that click-clack were actually Louis Vuitton shoes. And the bag, I recognize as this season's Chanel. I struggle to stifle a groan from the growing pain in my thigh caused by the sudden and violent spasms my wallet has gone into at the thought of it having to support the weight of such gifts, which I'm assuming she's become accustomed to on her birthday, Valentine's day, Christmas, New Year's, or any general girlfriend-appreciation day. There is a brief shudder at the thought that she can probably afford to buy those types of things on her own as well. (Damn! She outearns me!) As she was a "seven" or "eight" from afar, she's definitely a "ten" or "eleven" up close! My heart rate speeds up, hands become clammy, I start stammering my words, and fear has taken root! I manage to mutter a "Well, it was nice meeting you," as I end the conversation prematurely and scurry off back to the confines of my comfy chair, thus dodging the brutal savagery of a rejection from a perfect "ten."

B. *Definite interest!* Because what I notice as we chat is that she's very open, friendly, and quite witty and clever. Jackpot! Her outfit is even more tasteful up close than from afar, and striding atop those click-clackity heels are two of the most professionally and sexily pedicured feet I've ever seen! If this goes well, I'm gonna have to change my plans for the next weekend.

C. *Possible interest.* Because while she's very cute, she's not as hot as I initially thought. Smart enough at first, just not terribly engaging. The nails on the hands and feet could use some work, and the hair could stand a fresh visit to the salon. Body is still great and definitely stylish enough. Surely not one I'd throw back for now. I'll run her through my player-development program and see just how she might be of use to my team!

D. *No interest!* Because upon further inspection, those feet that caused the clatter actually look like they've spent a lifetime kicking things and walking barefoot on large expanses of rough ground. The makeup is so ridiculous I can't tell if she's going to a party or to a circus! And I have yet to discern one complete sentence expressing anything that resembles a thought from her! Can't play with it! Can't win with it! Can't coach it! I'll just move on. Damn! I hope nobody stole my chair!

Answer: B. *Definite interest!* Ladies, ever have one of those chance encounters that leave you walking away with a smile? Well, that's what we just had. It was light, witty, and respectful. She obviously takes pride in her appearance and recognizes that in me as well. While we don't know each other's "situation," as yet, this could be the beginning of a beautiful friendship and maybe more!

2. Okay, ladies, it's the end of a long workweek, and you're ready to unwind. You've been single and loving it for a while and just want to have fun with your girls this weekend. You call up your main girl, who is newly single, and decide to meet up at this new upscale martini bar you've heard about. Both you and your girl are quite stunning (or at least that's what you've been told a time or two … hundred). You've got your Beyonce Knowles "freak'em dress" on, and she has on her best "fuck'em dress" (again, because she's newly single). You're having a delightful time and enjoying each other's company when it happens. In he walks. Hotness in male form! Sunshine in an Armani suit! Tall, handsome, and built like a linebacker in the NFL. Damn! And he seems to have noticed you right away. No matter, you and your girl acknowledge it and move on. You're both quite adept at handling these types of situations. So Sunshine (we don't know his name yet) makes a beeline for you and asks if the seat at the bar next to you is taken. "No? Then may I please sit?" Of course. As Sunshine slides into his chair, he places his keys on the bar, and you notice the monogram MP on his French cuffs. Must stand for Mr. Perfect! Because before you saw the monogram, you noticed there was no ring on his finger. You also notice his keys—one with the unmistakable encircled three-pronged star of a Mercedes. The other you're not so familiar with. A rather understated key except it's fire engine red and has a picture of a horse on it. Your girl squeezes your leg in what can be regarded as a death grip as she leans over and informs you that that is, in fact, a key to a Ferrari … or as she likes to call it ... heaven! The conversation ensues and is quite polite and funny, and he has offered to buy the next round of drinks for you and your friend. He is flirting openly with you but keeping her included in the conversation as well. You politely excuse yourself to the little girls' room. *Wow! He even stands when you leave the table!* When you return, you notice your girl has slid over one stool next to him, and they seem to be having a spirited conversation. You're welcomed back into the fold, but the mood seems to have changed just a bit. The conversation is definitely more geared toward the three of you. And even though you thought you all were having a delightful time, he suddenly excuses himself and bids you ladies a good night. He didn't ask for either of your phone numbers, but he did inquire as to when would be the next time you may be at this particular martini bar. What just happened here, ladies? What's his level of interest and in whom?

What are the chances you will see Mr. Perfect again?

A. *Excellent.* Because while you and your girl when out together consistently seem to intimidate most mere males who feel you are out of their league, Mr. Perfect here not only seemed quite comfortable with the totality of your beauty but even excited by your presence as well.

B. *Excellent!* Because you thought he had definite interest in you. He was polite, asked pertinent but not prying questions, and seemed comfortable managing a situation with two beautiful women without making either of you feel uncomfortable. This one may be a keeper!

C. *Fair.* Because you thought he had possible interest that would have developed into definite interest had he not had some previous engagement for which he had to excuse himself early. You'll just have to make sure you are there when you told him you would be next time and take extra special care to make sure you're looking your most fetching.

D. *None!* Because what you don't know at this point is that while you were on your little bathroom break, Mr. Perfect and your best girl who's newly single seemed to hit it off quite well! Turns out his gym is fairly close to her job, and they agreed to meet for lunch one day next week. They exchanged numbers just in case either of them got lost ... awww ... how safe and sweet of both of them.

E. *Excellent.* But not in a good way. Because what neither of the women in this scenario realized was that Mr. Perfect here just ran the old divide and conquer game on the both of you. Two beautiful women together. Could possibly be interested in both but it's too soon to tell, as he doesn't know either of you just yet. Only way to remedy that is to get to know both of you. Separately! Lunch at this place, martinis at another, but never together. He made sure to arrange to meet each of you at this same bar, but at different times. He may even be so bold as to tell each of you about the other in the spirit of honesty. Be very careful here, ladies. This type of man has historically driven huge wedges in the relationships of girlfriends.

Answer: D. Girl! You know it's D! You know your girl is newly single and, not that she's the least bit sketchy, she does have a history of morally questionable behavior. I wouldn't call her that word that's overly used and starts with an "h," ends with an "o," and rhymes with "bo," but you have noticed strong tendencies toward that direction from her of late. Weeks later, she will justify it to you by saying "well, we met him at the same time, and you left the scene for a while, so I didn't think you were interested." Don't buy it! But at least you learned a couple of lessons. Lesson number one: never leave the field in the heat of battle. Lesson number two: never, ever, ever leave your girlfriends alone around your man or any man you may be interested in. If you thought that lightning strikes fast, it is downright turtlelike when compared to the blinding quickness of a "ho-strike"!

Note to those of you who thought the answer was E, congratulations ... now you're beginning to understand how the male mind really works ...

Getting to Know You

Okay, ladies, here is where I'm gonna ask you to do something that may be difficult for some of you. I'm gonna need you to change your way of thinking just a bit. It's gonna be tough because part of the wonderment of a new relationship is those waves of fun, light, can't wait to see you, can't wait to know more about you emotions. Those are good, so keep those, because in order for any relationship to last, there has to be that element of playfulness and innocence to it. But also, ladies, I need you to get more practical here. It's like poker. Eventually, you're gonna get to see all our cards; it's just a matter of when and how many cards we're gonna show you at one time. Every poker player has a "tell," and if you're good, you can pick up on it, and it will clue you in every time to what he's holding—either a great hand or pure garbage. Same with every guy you know. We all have a tell! Ladies, you just have to pay attention early and often to pick up on it. Believe me, it will make your dating life so much easier. Guys use much fewer words to express themselves. As a result, we tell more through our body language. At least 50 percent of human communication is nonverbal. That is to say, it comes from body language. For guys, it's probably a bit more. A nervous laugh, blinking eyes, mumbling, body posture, fidgeting hands, or tapping feet.

These are subtle little things that we do that clue you in that we're venturing into uncomfortable territory for us. That foreign uncomfortable place is typically a little non-extradition island just off the coast called "The Truth." Guys know where it is but rarely want to go for a visit. We can take you there if you really want to go, but we can't promise you're gonna have a good time once you get there. I say that to say this: here is where I'm gonna put the onus on you, ladies. You need to ask pertinent questions and actually listen (and look) at the answers. These answers will be your map to the truth. I have so many friends and also patients who come in and say, "I didn't know he was like that. I didn't know that's who he was." My response is usually the same: "Why didn't you know? Did you ask him? What did he tell you?"

Ladies, you can't be afraid to ask the meaningful questions. It's not all about his favorite color, favorite music or food, favorite place to travel, the kinds of clothes he likes to wear, or what he does for fun and relaxation. Those things are all well and good and are part of who he is, but they don't go to the core of a person. What you need are questions that get to the heart of who he is. What is the essence of him? And in the beginning, this is scary, in part, because no one wants to be too pushy and too intrusive too fast. And guys do so love their little secrets. The other part is that I think some of you don't ask the hard questions because, deep down, you don't want to be disappointed again. There is so much hope and anticipation wrapped up in the possibility of everything that could be with this guy, and there has usually been so much disappointment and regret with past relationships that it's only natural to want to avoid going there immediately. But you must. It will save you time and effort and countless numbers of telephone conversations over drinks with your girls trying to figure out "where he's coming from."

I hate to go all *Star Wars* on you here, ladies, but "search your feelings … you know this to be true." There are things you need to know about the man you are planning on dating, and some of these things are not pretty. Here are some questions that you really need the answer to, or you at least need to ask them in his presence, so you can see the type of bullshit ... excuse me ... type of reaction he gives you. For example, here are some typical questions that you need answers to, which guys routinely like to lie about. I've also provided you with some examples of "red flag" or worrisome answers and "white flag" or acceptable answers.

Are you married?

On the surface this is a fairly straightforward, simple, direct, and to-the-point kind of question. I am routinely amazed at the variations in answers women will accept. The one I hear the most is "yes, but I'm not happy." Well, no shit—name me one married man who truly is. Sorry, that's the frustration talking. Ladies, this is one of those few things in life that is truly black or white. It's like a light switch; either it's on or off. You should accept no in-between here. He may tell you he's separated or going through a divorce, or they are living separate but equal lives (which is a particularly interesting situation), married but unhappy, or my personal favorite lie: I'm planning on leaving her.

Ladies, women, sweetie pie, honey-bunch, please don't fall for it! Bottom line, as long as he's in a committed relationship in any way, shape, or form with someone else, he will never, I repeat, *never*, commit to you! Now, for some of you that may, in fact, be okay; you say, well, I'm not looking for a commitment anyway. But one year later, here you come crying to my office about how you fell for a married man and yada yada yada. This is a dangerous game to play, and it's one you will not win. My best clinical advice is to move on. You'll thank me; his unsuspecting wife will thank me; and your poor, dear, best girlfriend who would have had to endure countless hours of your venting about him will surely thank me.

Red flag answers:
- *He hesitates or looks away before answering.*
- Yes, but I'm not happy.
- We're going through a separation right now.
- We're living separate but equal lives right now.
- I'm only there physically; mentally, I've moved on.
- I'm thinking about leaving her. (An all-time favorite of guys!)
- Sigh, I think we just grew apart. (Or any other form of avoidance of your question.)
- I can't leave her because I still love her, but I'm just not *in love* with her. (Another classic lie!)

White flag answers:
- *He gives an immediate answer and maintains direct eye contact.*
- No. (Beautiful in its simplicity.)

Have you ever been married?

"Ummm …" define married. (That's a typical response.) Ladies, ask this question, and watch us squirm. Here's a tip: if we give you anything other than a one-word answer (as in "no"), then the answer is yes. Do not get lost in the details of the sob story! We know you are emotional creatures who are empathic and understanding by nature. We use that against you! Again, *lived with, stay with sometimes, never legally, never had a ceremony,* and *only for a little while* all qualify as a resounding yes. Be careful here, ladies. If you buy these little white lies, we know we have a bona fide "GG" (Gullible Girl) here, and there is no end or limit to the fantastic and amazing lies we will be able to tell you and have you believe throughout the course of our time together.

Red flag answers:
- Well, I wouldn't really call it a marriage.
- We were just together a really long time.
- I guess, by common law.

- I've lived with most of my girlfriends.
  (Interpretation: I plan on moving in with you, too,
  at some point, if you believe this!)
- No, but she took half of my stuff when we broke
  up, so we might as well have been. (Anger,
  frustration, resentment ... ladies, if you're lucky
  enough to get this answer, then consider yourself
  fortunate, and skip to your preferred mode of
  transportation of the day as you leave him and his
  baggage behind!)

White flag answers:
- Yes, divorced.
- No. (The point here is that this is a very simple
  question that requires only a very simple answer;
  any extended explanation should raise a red flag in
  your mind.)

Do you have any children?

Again, it's like a light switch. Either it's on or off. It's either
yes or no. *They don't live with me, they stay with their mother, they
don't live here, I don't see them, my mom takes care of them,* and
none that I'm claiming all qualify as a yes! Be careful here, ladies.
Consider this: if you pursue a relationship here, and by chance
sexual congress does occur ... and (gasp) you get pregnant, then
that may be your child whom one day he isn't claiming, taking
care of, or involving in his life. And at that point, it is irrelevant
whether you saw it coming or not; the damage will already have
been done, both to you and your child.

Red flag answers:
- *He shows any sign of hesitation or a shift in body
  language.*
- Do *you* have any kids? (This is just deflection ...
  don't fall for it!)
- Not that I know of.
- She said it was mine, but it didn't look like me!

- I don't see them so not really.
- My baby mama won't let me see them so not really. (Run! Run fast!)
- They already have a daytime daddy, so they don't really need me.
- *He utters any form of curse word or sigh at this point.*
- *He stares off into space, and his eyes well up with tears* (well … this reaction should be self-explanatory.)

White flag answers:

- Yes.
- Yes, and I see them every other weekend or at least once a month.
- *If the answer is yes, then any form of excitement or enthusiasm for his child or children at this point is a definite plus!*
- No.
- Hell, no!
- I hate kids! (This is an interesting response … may not be of immediate concern, but if this relationship progresses, then this will definitely be an issue in the future.)

Have you ever been to jail (as in, put in jail, not just bailing out a buddy)?

And if so, for what? (Believe me, a reckless driving speeding ticket is a helluva lot different than being there for a CDV (Criminal Domestic Violence charge). Here's what we like to say: "only for one night" (only acceptable if this were a Luther Vandross song, which clearly, it is not), or "my last girlfriend called the cops on me one night 'cause we were arguing, jus' cause I violated parole" (huge, ginormous red flag!), or "naw, but my last girlfriend had a court order against me 'cause she said she was scared of me." All lies! Ladies, run! Run fast! These are all thinly veiled ways of disguising criminal charges such as criminal domestic violence, stalking, restraining orders, orders of protection, and repeat offenders. Again, run fast! Here's the truth: leopards don't change their spots, and neither do guys. What we did then we are gonna continue to do now, only in varying ways. Ladies, you believe it can't happen to you only because it actually hasn't happened yet. It's human nature to believe that but foolish not to recognize it once you've been fairly warned. Oftentimes, these types of cases end poorly. Unfortunately, I've seen two deaths of young women in the last year who didn't think it could happen to them. I'm not saying people can't change. What I am saying is that I don't think you want to be the one at home alone, or at the bail bondsman's alone, or visiting him in prison alone, or lying in your hospital bed alone (there's a theme here) while we all wait for him to wake up one morning and decide it's time for him to change. Move on.

Red flag answers:

- Yes. (At least he didn't lie.)
- Not really in "jail" jail.
- Naw, just for a little while.
- Yeah, but it was bullshit, though.
- Yeah, but they had the wrong guy. (Classic!)
- I was going through some stuff and had to do what I had to do. (What the hell does this mean? Could be anything … just move on.)
- Not really, my ex was just crazy, and we used to get into it. (Battery … move on!).
- Yeah, but I've changed now.
- *The variety of answers here is infinite. Basically, anything other than a straight no means yes. I don't want to get into a rant here about the wonderfully rehabilitative powers of the U.S. penal system, but let me just say that the behaviors that led to his being jailed are typically ones that are hard to change, and I'm not sure it's wise for you to choose to start out a new relationship trip with this much added cargo.*

White flag answers:
- No.
- Well, there was this one time in college …
  (Everyone was young and foolish once, and
  I think something stupid but harmless like a
  horrible spring break story, excessive speeding,
  or mouthing off at a cop after a night of liquid-
  courage-building all qualify and are probably
  excusable.)

Have you ever had any legal problems?

Do you now or have you ever had any restraining orders against you (this ties in to the above question)?

Or better yet, say "I'm planning a little getaway for us. Are there any places you can't legally go at this time?" Guys fall for this carrot every time, because we are only interested in the reward (kinda like a little kid) and will clumsily knock over and spill all types of truths about ourselves to get it.

Red flag answers:
- Ummm … define legal.
- None that I care to discuss.
- Not anymore … thank God!
- The Lord blessed me to walk away from that life.
- *Any cute quip that avoids your question is a definite red flag!*

White flag answers:
- No.
- Nothing my lawyer couldn't handle. (Then he
  explains … again, everyone is allowed a screwup
  or two, but it shouldn't become a pattern of
  behavior!)

Are you gay or bisexual?
Red flag answers:
- Yes. (Damn, but he's such a great guy! I know, I

know. At least he was honest.)
- I used to be.
- I hate faggots! (Much too ignorant! Much too emotional! Move on.)
- Why, yes, I sometimes enjoy the touch of a warm man … and woman … on a cold night. (Again, at least he didn't lie about it. I don't want to get off on a rant here, but let me say this: I believe everyone has a right to choose whatever lifestyle he or she prefers and should be respected for that choice. What you have to do, ladies, is decide exactly where you fit into this lifestyle, and if it's honestly going to be one that is conducive to your having a lasting, meaningful, monogamous relationship with this guy.)

White flag answers:
- No.

Ladies, the answer to this question is often meaningless, because we are going to answer it only in the context of the here and now—as in, at this moment here today, talking with you right now, no, I'm not gay. What you're really looking for here is his reaction and how visibly uncomfortable he gets when you ask this question (some guys may even get a momentary twinkle in their eyes and twitch in their nether regions as the memory of the last bout of man on man action leaps to the forefront of their minds), so ask this question instead:

Have you ever had sex with a man?

There is no such thing as experimentation or going through a phase or not being sure about oneself. A yes here is a yes … period! It is what it is, ladies. Remember my light switch; it's either on or off. Now, this brings us to an interesting topic. What must be done with the gay or bisexual male? Is there a chance of his being useful to you ladies in the normal constraints of a typical relationship? And again, I'm going to put the onus on you ladies. If a man has the guts to tell you the truth about this situation, then you have to be honest enough with yourself to know exactly how you feel about it. Some women are okay with their husbands being openly gay, as these women have no interest in them sexually, and if those needs are present, she will obviously be filling that void (ha, I made a funny) elsewhere. These women simply want the show or the pretext of marriage; here, it's all about appearances. Then there's what I like to call "ATL-itis." You know how there seems to be a very large number of gay, bisexual, and down-low or in-the-closet men in Atlanta (commonly referred to as "A-T-L") in proportion to the very small number of single, very eligible heterosexual women. Women are inventing new ways to accept and wrap their minds around what is going on there. Ladies, this is where you start lying to yourself. You say, "I didn't know he was still gay (still gay?). He said he had gotten born again and wasn't like that anymore. He said it was just a phase, and he was just curious that one time. I didn't know he wouldn't change." All lies—of course you knew, because he told you. Then I told you, remember, the best predictor of future behavior is past behavior. You know, the old leopard and its spots thing.

In medical school, I learned that the proper name for an anus that has never been penetrated is "the untutored anus." Ladies, some of you perceive your situation as being so desperate that not only are you willing to deal with men whose anuses have been properly tutored, but also some of you are willing to deal with guys whose anuses have passed the class, graduated from college, and gone on to get PhDs! Stop doing that! It's not gonna make you happy. One of the saddest things I've ever heard come out of a woman's mouth was when she, a suicidal fifty-eight-year-old woman said she just didn't trust and was no longer okay with her husband (who did not lie about being openly gay and stated he would continue to receive … tutoring … on occasion before they got married) having his male friends anymore, after thirty years of marriage. She looked so utterly defeated and with nothing to show for it. Well, I told her she can take away from the marriage the good times and closeness of companionship they had shared, at least. But the time she now feels she lost is just that—lost. Because she wasn't honest with herself at the outset. Little lies become big lies—sometimes really fast, sometimes slowly and tragically.

Red flag answers:

- Yes.
- Yes, but just that one time.
- Yes, but I didn't like it.
- Well, he did me, but I didn't really do him.
- Yes, and it was wonderful!
- I'm not sure; I was kinda drunk.
- Does oral count?
- No, we just kind of held each other.

White flag answers:

- No.
- No, but I think Tyson Beckford and Hugh Jackman are hot! (Alas, who doesn't? Nothing wrong with a man being able to acknowledge another man being handsome.)

When's the last time you went on a date?

"Oh, a few months ago." "It's been awhile. I can't remember the last time I went out on a date." (This one is particularly cute, because we will actually smile while we tell you this, and we're smiling because we are remembering the great time we had the last time we went on that date you just asked us about.) Rare is the guy who answers this question honestly. Because to do that means we are going to have to have other answers that accurately match up with the those related questions like "when was your last girlfriend? How long were y'all together? When did y'all break up?" An honest answer here means we must be prepared to answer all those other questions in that line honestly as well. And let's face it: that's gonna start to get really messy really fast. But ladies, you must ask. You must know if you're dealing with a serial dater here. You know, someone who dates just for the sake of company for dinner and possible nakedness later versus someone who is simply single and dating, looking for a connection. Serial daters go out on weekly dates, sometimes several a week as compared to single guys who are honestly looking for someone to make a real connection with and may date two to three times a month. Then there are some guys who truthfully have been dating about as often as a lot of married men I know are having passionate intimate sex … alas … not much, if ever.

Red flag answer:
- Today.
- Last night.
- Define date.
- I don't know. How often do you date? (Again, deflection … don't fall for it.)
- It's been awhile since I've gone on a good one.
- Hard to say, really … (Translation: I'm not really good at keeping such complicated schedules in my head. Further translation: he's been dating a lot!)
- Honestly … (Ironically enough, most sentences that men begin with the word "honestly" rarely contain honesty.)

White flag answer:
- Last week.
- Last weekend.
- Last month.
- I usually go on a few dates a month on average. (Any realistic time frame here, ladies, is acceptable. Think about how often you or your girlfriends date, and it will be about the same for guys.)

Are you dating anyone now?
Red flag answers:

- Not right this moment.
- Oh, nothing serious.
- *Beware if you see any weird looks on his face as he thinks about how unhappy he is with the person he's actually dating right now, especially right before he tells you no.*
- I was, but we kinda drifted apart. (Translation: Yes, but I'm not really liking her right now and would gladly break up with her for a better option.)
- No. I mean, I go out on dates, but I'm not actually *dating* anyone.
- I have someone I hang out with and kick it with from time to time.
- I have female friends I enjoy doing different things with, but we're just friends. (While this is not entirely impossible, it's such a rarity for a man to have a female friend whom he actually has not and has no intention of sleeping with. An answer like this should definitely give you pause.)

White flag answers:

- I have someone I've been getting to know recently.
- I've been seeing someone, but I'm not sure how serious it may become.
- Yes.
- No. *(*Again, it's a relatively simple question, so the answer should reflect the same.)

This question is similar to the question above it but very different in meaning to us guys. And again, the question holds little meaning for us guys, because at this moment right here talking with you, the answer is clearly no. Last night, however, is a different story, so ask this one instead:

Is there anyone you are currently in a sexual relationship with now or within the last month?

There's where the rubber meets the road! Now you're askin' some damn fine questions, ladies, if I do say so myself. Guys will be put off initially by the cleverly crafted nature of that question. More mature guys will secretly admire that question for its clarity of purpose—which is basically to ask *Who are you fuckin'?* Hold his feet to the fire here, ladies. Squirm as he might, he must give you an answer here. It's critical for you to know, so you can decide for yourself if you will be among the *coalition of the willing* or if you will simply continue to get to know this man but keep him "out of cock's reach."

Red flag responses:
- *He laughs.*
- *He coughs.*
- *He sighs.*
- *He shifts position.*
- *He shakes his head.*
- *Any hesitation.*

White flag answers:
- Yes. (Then he may explain, or you can ask him how serious it is.)
- No.

Do you have anything that I might catch?

As in, a sexually transmitted disease, a court case because you dabble in activities that are legally questionable, or a mean left hook to the jaw because of a crazy ex-girlfriend.

Again, ladies, if he's a good guy, he will tell you the truth. What you're looking for is his reaction. Such a direct question will give him pause while he decides if he should tell you the truth or not—typically this takes from two to five seconds. Use that time wisely to gather your belongings and leave, or if on the telephone with him, mistakenly end that call. The truth here will come immediately. If the answer is no, then you will more than likely not even be able to finish this question before he blurts out a "hell, no." Now, that's not to say that you still shouldn't be careful just because he puts your mind at ease verbally. I had an ob-gyn instructor in medical school who always preached to us the importance of "looking before you touch." He would say, "For God's sakes, folks, pull the sheets back, and turn the lights on before you go down there for any activity. You gotta see what's going on!" Funny as hell and oh so true. Unfortunately, today a lot of STDs don't show any physical signs, so even looking doesn't confirm anything. The savvy dater will request "papers" or recent evidence from someone's doctor that he or she is indeed disease free. A very sticky subject to broach but one that can save you a lifetime of explanations, headaches, and embarrassment. The most common sexually transmitted diseases do not go away ever!

Red flag answers:

- What do you mean?
- As in right now?
- No, not anymore.
- Naw, I took care of that.
- Yeah, but somebody gave it to me. I didn't give it to her.
- Sometimes, but it's just because I hate wearing condoms. I like that all natural kind of feeling.
- Yes, but you can't tell anything.

White flag answers:

- No.
- Hell, no!
- Yes, unfortunately. It's being treated. (Be very careful here, ladies. You may even need to go home and do a little research about the disease and figure out if this is someone you're willing to risk your health for.)

Where are you from?

Here, ladies, you want to get a feel for what he was exposed to as child. The truth is that chivalry is not dead, and men from certain areas or regions pride themselves on just that. Southern gents open car doors and pull out chairs for their lady folk (usually). Guys from more urban areas tend to want to impress you more with how worldly they are and the things they would like to experience with you. But again, there are guys who don't fit the mold here, and the truth is, it's not so much where he's from but what he was exposed to as a child that will govern his interactions with you. If he's seen his dad open a door for his mom, then chances are, he will do the same for you. On the other hand, if he's seen his father be less than gentle with his mom, chances are that he has learned a pattern of behavior that will be hard to break. And you don't want him to be breaking anything on you, correct? Here's the truth: we do what we know. What we know is what we have seen and been exposed to. It takes the most extraordinary of leopards to change his spots and, quite frankly, there just aren't that many leopards with squares or triangles running around out there.

Red flag answers:

- There was this one time, back home, when my dad chased my mom out of the house with his gun …
- I like women who wear shades a lot; it reminds me of my mom back home. She had to wear shades all the time because she always had bruises around her eyes …
- We moved a lot growing up. My mom's boyfriend's used to walk all over her …
- In my country, women are seen and not heard and always walk ten paces behind the man. (However, if he happens to be from a place you're unfamiliar with, then it would definitely be in your best interest to do a little due diligence and familiarize yourself! Also, guys like to use the last place they

lived as where they're from sometimes, so a better
way to get the information you want is to ask us
where we grew up.)

White flag answers:

- *Just about any answer here will do. You just want to
  make sure it's where he spent the majority of his time,
  and if that time was divided frequently, then ask
  which place he liked or disliked the most (these will
  be the places that had the greatest impact on him).
  Again, the goal here is to get an idea of what this man
  has been exposed to or seen up until this point in his
  life. You want to get information that reinforces the
  idea that he was exposed to an environment in which
  he saw men treat women with respect.*

Do you have a family?

Big question, ladies. Pay very close attention to what we do
and say here, and if there are any evident pained looks on our
faces. Remember, you're applying for one of the open positions
of family member, possibly, so look alive. How we feel about
our families bears directly on how we are gonna feel about you.
I have five sisters, and I love them all dearly and never want to
see anything bad happen to them. As a result, my instincts in
relationships tend to be more nurturing and protective (awwww,
that's so sweet, I know, but focus; this ain't about me; it's about
you …). Seriously, we all have roles and places in a family.
What birth order did he fall in? The firstborn is very different
from the middle child or the baby. The science of birth order
is very fascinating and oh so evident in our everyday lives. The
firstborn child is often "the hero." As in "can do no wrong," no
matter how much wrong he or she actually does. Sometimes it's
the reverse, and the firstborn child becomes the scapegoat or
the easy target to blame for all that goes wrong with any other
children in the family. The firstborn child often has a certain
sense of entitlement that becomes readily apparent once you

understand the dynamics of the family. The middle child is oftentimes the lost or invisible child who often gets overlooked and often feels taken for granted. Unfortunately, this can lead to the middle child taking some extreme measures to get attention from people in their lives. The baby—well, he or she is just that … the baby! Often coddled, often praised. The baby's behavior is also often excused, no matter how unacceptable it may be. Were we always the screwup or always the good one? It matters because whoever we were in that family system is usually who we are gonna be in your family system … meaning in your relationship with us. I can't stress this enough.

Ladies, you need to take a good history here. The best tool to assess this, ladies, is to actually make a trip to his home when his family is there. That way, you can see how he interacts with them and, more importantly, how they interact (or don't interact) with him. Typical family members' behavior when meeting the new girlfriend is to tell cute but embarrassing stories about him. If those stories make reference to his being suspended from school, put in jail, "going away for a while," "needing to find himself," or needing to grow up, then run, ladies. Also be very leery of the overly friendly or overly inviting family. Family members know us for exactly who we are. Any guy whose mom or family seems all too ready to send you two down the aisle because "you're so good for him," you need to be very cautious of, because they know his path has been less than straight and narrow in the past, and they're hoping you will take the mantle of keeping it more straight from now on.

Again, ladies, you cannot change him! You cannot fix him! I know, I know; if you could, he'd be such the perfect guy—but he's not. It is what it is! He can only do these things for himself, if and when he's ready. You could attempt to help him with whatever issues he has, but rare is the guy who can truly appreciate that or you for trying. It's frustrating for you, because you see the good in him, but understand this: you would be trying to correct a pattern of behavior that has been occurring for most of his life. He needs a good therapist and possibly a psychiatrist to help with that, not another new girlfriend. Move on.

Red flag answers:
- I don't see them much.
- We're not close.
- Not really.
- Fuck 'em!
- No, it's just me. I'm so lonely. Will you be my family? (Just run!)

White flag answers:
- Yes. (And then some elaboration on whom they're close to and why and how often they see them. The truth is, we all have a family somewhere. They may or may not be biologically related, but they had a hand in raising and caring for us (or not). What you want to do is get an idea of what kind of value he puts on family, as it may have direct bearing on the value he places on you.)

Do you like kids?

Honest answer: "Not even my own!" I'm sorry; that came out all wrong. Let me rephrase. "I don't mind them. I know I'm just not ready for any of my own yet." Ladies, this is an important question for a couple of reasons. One: a man's like or dislike of children often reflects his own thoughts and feelings about if he thinks he will be a good father or not. Guys who are unsure of their paternal instincts will often say they don't want kids. Two: how quickly we give you the proverbial "hell, naw" answer to this question should clue you in as to whether we ever plan on having any kids with you, regardless of if we love children or not. And lastly, ladies, since we are being honest with each other here … a little *quid pro quo* … please ask this question because you are genuinely interested in the answer, not as a tool to gauge if and when you're gonna tell us that you actually already have one or two (or ten) children of your own! It hurts I know; it'll pass soon.

Red flag answers:

- *Beware of any blatant signs of anger mixed with unintelligible mumbling under his breath.*
- Little rug rats!
- Little hellions!
- I hate kids!
- No, my childhood was so awful, and my parents did such a poor job raising us that I don't think I could ever trust myself with raising a child of my own. (Yikes! On the one hand, you can commend his blatant honesty … with the other hand, you should be waving good-bye! This person sounds like he needs a therapist, not a girlfriend, baby mama, or wife.)

White flag answers:

- Yes
- Yes, I love kids but I know I'm not ready to have any yet.

Are you close to your mother?

This may be the single most important question you ask your new beau-to-be! The way a man treats his mother has direct bearing on how he will treat you. I repeat, the way a man feels about, talks about, and treats his mother has direct bearing on how he will feel about, talk about, and ultimately treat you! Ladies, if his answer to this question starts with anything less than flattering, that's not a good sign. On the other hand, if he speaks of his mom with reverence and love and smiles when he talks about her, then that is hugely favorable! Fond loving feelings toward his mom translate to fond loving feelings about most women in his life, which translate directly to fond, loving, caring, "would never hurt you" feelings about you! See how that works? Simple, right? Now, these are two extremes here, and you clearly want someone more on the latter end of this scenario than the former, but how will you know if you don't ask the question?

Red flag answers:
- Me and my mom never really got along. (Walk away.)
- My mom was never really there for me much. (Walk away quickly.)
- My mom's got some issues.
- I hate that f*cking bitch! (Run! Fast and hard, ladies. Put the wind to your backs, and get to the neighboring zip code as fast as something with wheels will carry you. Delete his number from your phone, block his e-mail, do not accept his calls at your job; there is no future here! Typically, in two or five or ten years, you, or you and your daughter, will be that proverbial "f*cking bitch" that he has transferred his hate to. Hop along, Cassidy. It's just not worth it.)

White flag answers:
- Yes.
- Love her to death!
- I can't imagine not being close to her.
- She's my best friend.

Are you close to your father?

Again, extremely important question here. Why? Because fathers are the people who teach boys how to be men. Correction—good fathers are the people who teach young boys how to be grown men. Have you ever seen that show on the Discovery channel where the baby ducks are learning how to walk and swim by following the mama duck, usually in a straight line? That's usually how it works with fathers and sons. Sons pattern themselves after the patterns and tendencies of our fathers. It's uncanny how this happens; sometimes it will be right down to the way he walks, talks, dresses, and even laughs. So, a guy's relationship with his father is extremely pertinent to you, ladies, as at some point, you might be considering his becoming a father to your children.

Red flag answers:

- I never knew my dad. (Strongly consider walking away. There's no amount of boy's clubbing, big brothering, group homing, or mentoring that will fill this void. Sad but true. It's not a void you can fill either. It's one he should have dealt with before he met you, to become ready to move on with the rest of his life. But all is not lost here. There are a large number of guys who come from this type of background, who have gone on to do extremely well both personally and professionally. Ladies, look at the whole picture here. If he's late in life and still struggling with consistency and impulsivity, then you could be looking at a man who hasn't reconciled with his past yet. However, if he has clearly gone on to do good things and has built a stable and productive life, then you could be looking at one of the few men who has effectively dealt with those father issues and auto-corrected or auto-filled the void left by the absent dad.)
- My dad was a f*cking asshole! (Please refer to the above explanation of the mom question and answer, of her being "a f*cking bitch." It seems pretty obvious to me, but I am amazed and confused at exactly how many people just don't get this concept. A family that has spawned these types of attitudes that a man would actually verbalize, is so inherently fraught with

dysfunction that you do not want any part of it! Move on! Because, guess what? If he thinks his dad was a "fucking asshole," what do you think he thinks of his mom, who chose to be with that fucking asshole? See where this is going? Exactly, nowhere for you, except maybe to Starbucks and Blockbuster *on your way home*, to have a latte and to watch a good movie and salvage what is left of this evening. I'm assuming here that you did indeed take my advice and walk away after he made his revelations to you.)

- My dad's in jail (Come on, do I really need to even say it? Why are you still there? Do you really need to hear what he's going to say next? No! Ladies, find the next thing smoking, and get on it and get the hell away! If you cannot find something with wheels leaving his presence directly, then call a good girlfriend and have her extract you! You know, that old "my girlfriend is having an emergency" routine ... you know what I'm talking about, ladies. Here's the truth: people in jail or who have gone to jail often have antisocial tendencies. They are prone to lying, stealing, violence, and insane levels of selfishness. These elements to their personality are both learned and passed along genetically. However he may have happened upon these unfortunate personality quirks is irrelevant to you because you will be moving on! Right? Note: there is a particular genre of women out there who tend to date only men in jail or men who frequent jail; this book is not for you! You actually need to pick up the book on the adjacent shelf entitled *My Man's a Hoodlum: The Bliss of Dating in Ignorance* by Spike "The Hammer" Jenkins.)

White flag answers:
- Yes!
- Love him to death!
- I can't imagine not being close to him.
- He's my best friend.

I've used some extreme emotions with both the mom and dad closeness questions, understanding that rarely does life occur in these extremes. The point is that a guy should have an overall positive attitude about both of them, and if he does not, then it may be necessary to explore why.

Where do you live?

Fairly innocent question here, ladies; it is what it is. You just want to know where he is in life and what his efforts have afforded him (and subsequently, what they may afford you). Note, the question is not where he *used to live* or where he is *about to be living*. Again, the question is where he lives now … today … as in, where his stuff is, right at this moment. A man with nothing to hide will love for you to see his place. On the other hand, a man with secrets will also be secretive about his residence. If you two will be going out, he will always want to "meet you there." Understand, a guy who doesn't have much may actually be ashamed of where he lives, and that may be the reason why he won't take you there. That's acceptable, and he need not apologize for this. But you still need to see the place. Again, look at the whole picture; a guy's residence is a part of who he is. Just because a man is from the hood doesn't mean he is of the hood! Conversely, just because a man is living in a mini-mansion in the hills doesn't mean his character is just as lofty. The other thing, ladies, is that seeing his place really gives you a sense of his style. Things that are important to us we keep close. Things that are important to us we display. Nothing like seeing where a guy lives to really get a clearer picture of who he is and what he feels is important in his life. It really helps complete the picture of him.

Red flag answers:
- You just make a left up there and keep straight. (Much too vague, and history has proven that the words "keep straight" in regards to where someone lives are very ominous!)
- With friends. (See below.)
- I'm kinda in between places right now.
- I'm staying with my mama and them right now.
- I just moved back in with my folks.
- I just sold my place. (Okay, so where do you live now? Answer the question, damn it!)
- I'm still staying with my ex until I get back on my feet.
- With my baby mama, so I can see my kid. (Or kids, or whatever! Looks like the start of a new country here—drama nation!)

White flag answers:
- Oh yes, dear girl, I live in the penthouse on the corner of Baller's Row and You-can't-afford-to-live-here Drive. (Followed by a haughty chuckle … nice … but would be much nicer if there was some humility about him, though.)
- It's not the best part of town. (That's okay, and you should definitely not make him feel bad about it. It is what it is, and you still want to get a look at the place.)
- Oh, I live [insert wherever in town here]. I'd love for you to see my place sometime.

Do you have any roommates?

This question is relative to his station in life. If he's in college, then a roommate is perfectly normal. If he's just out of school and just getting started, again, perfectly acceptable. If he's thirty-five, working (or not), clubbing on weekends, and vacationing in the summer and still has a roommate … then

... "Houston, we have a problem!" I take strong issue with a grown-ass man having a roommate or roommates. Firstly, it goes against his ability to live independently. Are there some issues with poor decision making? Are there employability issues? The question here, ladies, is why? Why does a grown-ass man need a roommate? Is the area expensive to live in, and a roommate helps keep the bills paid? Understandable; however, my advice would be to reduce your bills. Live within your means. I know grown men who right now today are living with three other roommates in two-bedroom apartments, gainfully employed, wearing the latest fashions, all driving current year model luxury cars ... ballin' (just ballin' with roommates)! What is this about? How screwed up are these guys' priorities? Ladies, I see a pattern of impulsive or just plain bad decision making here. Don't you become a part of that pattern ... move on. Again, ladies, look at the whole picture. Refer to the above question about where he lives. If he's in Atlanta or San Francisco, then men having "roommates" may be quite a common occurrence (just like having routine man-on-man sex may be a common occurrence for some men in those cities as well). Ladies ... ladies ... look at the obvious. It's ... well ... obvious! Look, men enjoy their solitude and their space. (Think Superman's fortress of solitude; think Batman in the bat cave.) No man willingly invites other men to share that private space with him unless he really, really needs to or unless he really, really enjoys sharing space with other men. Either way, it's a huge problem for you and not one you should probably tackle (unless you're willing to spring for his rent every month or share him with his "best friend who's having hard times right now" Oh, the lies we do tell!).

Red flag answers:

- Yes. (Depends on the explanation.)
- I'm just crashing at a friend's place for now.
- Yeah, I live with Steve and them.
- For sure! Gotta stay with my boys!

- Yeah, gosh, if Antonio moved out and left me.
  I'd just feel lost. (Hmmm … methinks we have a
  problem here!)
- Yeah, but they're just there in the daytime.

White flag answers:
- Yes. (Depends on the explanation.)
- No.

Are you working right now?

As in, come Monday morning, is there anywhere you need
to be in order to receive a paycheck on Friday?

The intent here is fairly obvious, or at least it should be. Do
you have a j-o-b or not? Ladies, if you do not mind supporting
him (having a man depend on you for money), then go right
ahead and ignore this question. In the beginning, you may even
find it cute to help him out, all the while assuming he will be so
appreciative once he comes through this. Think again! Rarely
does that happen, and it is naïve of you to think that your
situation is different. It's not. It's the same. This is the same
tired as hell game that deadbeat guys have been running on
overly willing women since the beginning of time. It only stops
when you make it stop. Here's the truth: If he isn't working
when you meet him, chances are he won't be working when
you leave him. Sorry. It goes to the core of a man. Most men
are brought up with the values of being able to provide for
their families or, at the very least, themselves. Unless your new
friend is independently wealthy and thus does not require a
paycheck, his being unemployed is and should be a problem for
you! Ladies, to a good man, there is nothing more infuriating
than seeing a woman show up for work in her nice clothes
and her nice car and then watching her man get out from the
passenger's side in some form of sweat pants, flip-flops, socks,
T-shirt (basically any form of "I won't be going to work today"
clothes), walk around to the driver's side, and drive his sorry ass
back home to watch *Maury*! Now, this sounds very cold, I know,

and lots of people have legitimate reasons for being out of work and probably won't be unemployed for long, but in this book we are attempting to deal in the here and now. The "what is," not the "what could be." His not working today means you pay for dinner, you pay for gas, you pay for trips, you pay for movies, and, yes, the popcorn too … and "oh, hey, baby, you think you could lend me five hundred dollars to pay my rent?" Damn! Why? Is the dating scene that desperate? Really? Ladies, this is not a man; it simply bears a strong likeness to one. In reality, this is more like a child—at best, an overly developed teen. Ladies, if you want a child, then get pregnant, carry the child for nine months, and then give birth. Believe me, it's much faster and much less painful. If you want a man, find one who's working! This is an easy one; let's just move on.

Red flag answers:
- I'm out of work right now.
- The market is slow.
- Just in a rough patch.
- I'm rethinking some things.
- I'm kinda in between jobs right now. (Next question: do you get paid in-between money?)
- I'm having some issues with my boss right now. (What's the issue? He or she is the boss, and you're not … end of issue.)

White flag answers:
- Yes.
- Yes, part-time.
- No, but I go on what seems like a thousand interviews a week.

That car you were driving the other day sure was nice; was it yours?

Ha, good luck getting a straight answer here! Hell, I've even thought about lying about this one. It's such an easy and tempting lie to tell. After all, cars can be such fleeting objects.

Why, anything could happen to my car between now and the next time I may see you. It's shameful, I know. And just why are you so interested in what I drive anyway? Is that all you're concerned about? Is that the type of person you are? See how us guys like to turn that one around on you? Easy, right? Don't fall for it! The truth is something more like "it's actually a rental" or "it's actually my friend's car" (heads up, ladies; that would be his more mature, more stable, financially secure, usually better-looking friend's car). What we drive is what we drive. Men are creatures of habit, and our driving habits should not change that quickly. If they do, that is highly suspect of an underlying, more unstable situation.

Red flag answers:

- Yeah, but it got stolen.
- Yeah, but I wrecked it, and it was totaled. (Liars always like to add a little bit extra at the end.)
- Yeah, but I just put it in storage.
- Yeah, but I'm letting (whomever) drive it right now.
- Yeah, but I sold it.
- Yeah, but I only use it on weekends and maybe holidays. (See the little bit extra?)
- Yeah, me and my roommates share it.
- Kinda. It's my baby's mama's car, but she lets me use it, (Holy shit! You shouldn't still be listening after he said "baby's mama's car"!)

White flag answers:

- Why, thank you, yes!

Do you have any bad habits?

More than you have cute fingers and toes, my dear. But none I'm gonna tell you! Why should I tell you now? It ruins the fun of your finding out slowly and painfully on your own. I'll save those little pearls until after you have feelings for me, and then you will find it increasingly hard to leave me. At least, that's the plan anyway. I think we're all guilty of this lie at some point in the relationship. Both because we don't want to lose what could be and because we really do believe that we can change some of those bad habits … "if only I had a good woman (or man) to help me." Get real. They're called habits for a reason. Because you do them often, repeatedly, as in, a lot, and you have been doing them for a long time now and, to this point, have seen no reason to adjust your behavior. I agree with one of my best friends, a psychologist, who says "the best predictor of future behavior is past behavior." Sage wisdom. Simple, but true. Ladies, if you met me drinking and smoking at a club riding "wit my boys," then guess where I'm gonna be on Saturday night six months from now, regardless of if we're together or not?

Red flag answers:

- Nope, none!

White flag answers:

- Sure.
- Just a few.
- None that get me into trouble.

Two of my nephews, who are currently in college and fancy themselves rappers, who in this case actually have some aptitude for it ,as they have amazing lyrics with soulful beats and volumes of material that you can check out online when you search for NSC or NevaSoberCrew (shameless plug), but I digress … anyway … they have a song that's called "Mr. Tell'em What They Wanna Hear." It's a song about getting dolled up, going out to a nightclub, and entertaining the possibilities of the evening. These are some of the lyrics:

> My mission is clear
> Together me and you we leavin' here
> What you tell 'em man?
> Anything they wanna hear!
> Game strong like German Beer

We headin' to the spot like ... Yeah!

Tell'em what they wanna hear!

Ladies, you have to understand that, in the initial stages of meeting you, our mission is very clear. We are going to tell you exactly whatever it is we think you need to hear in order for us to progress to whatever level relationship we already plan to take you to. Have you ever had one or two conversations, ladies, with your new friend, and then you have come away thinking how lovely and long the conversations were, but on afterthought, you realize you really didn't find out that much about him? Do you think that was by accident? No! It was art. Simply beautiful. The art of telling you everything without telling you anything—or anything meaningful. Not lying, but crafting the truth. Guys are simple craftsmen, really; some of us are masters of our trade! As any fine craftsman, we need our trusty tools of the trade. One of those tools—telling lies!

I've given a lot of examples here; some may sound familiar to you, and some may not. The point is to get you in the frame of mind of asking tough questions and paying strict attention to the answers. Questions that count. Questions that matter. Questions that, depending on the answer, are going to make a real difference in any relationship.

Pop Quiz:

1. You're in Bed Bath and Beyond at 11:45 on a Sunday morning. There is an incredibly cute guy looking quite bewildered as he searches through the 1.2 million shower curtains on display. What do you do?

A. Approach and offer a cute word of encouragement and advice (i.e., hit on him)?

B. Watch from afar for a few minutes to see if a significant other approaches, or if he gives a distress call to someone.

C. Pass him by in disgust, as he seems routinely drawn to

only the most hideous of designs, which probably means he has no taste and could never be someone you would be interested in anyway.

D. None of the above.

Answer: D. None of the above! Why? Because clearly there are damn few single, heterosexual men who are gonna roll out of bed on a Sunday morning to drag their unshaved and probably hungover asses to Bed Bath and Beyond! Come on, ladies, that's a no-brainer! Pay attention to the obvious! People will tell you so much about themselves before you ever need to ask a single question or say hi. He is there either because he really, really wants to be there or because someone (e.g., his wife or girlfriend) made him go. If he really, really wants to be there, clearly this man had a hard-on for shower curtains all day Saturday and couldn't wait to get to the store Sunday morning, so he could pick one out, take it home, and try it out in his bathroom. Sorry, ladies. Not only does this guy not play for your team, but he's also not even playing the same sport. He's playing stickball when you simply wanted to play catch! Sorry ... lame joke, I know. If he is being forced to go, it's pretty much the same end result for you: no hope of advancement. He is otherwise unavailable, and the frustrated look on his face should tell you as much.

2. You've been hearing more and more about this new guy in the HR department at work. He's thirty-eight years old, new in town, newly single, no children, lives alone, and apparently has an eye for fashion, as he's quite the sharp dresser. You two have exchanged glances a few times and have had a few conversations about things to do in town. It's quite obvious that there is mutual attraction and interest, so how do you proceed?

A. Immediately give him your cellular number, e-mail, and MySpace user ID. No sense in wasting time; let's get this

love thing in motion!
B. Find out what times and where he usually has lunch and just happen to bump into him at that time. You may be able to further your conversations and see how mutual this attraction goes.
C. Wait, and if he does invite you out to lunch or dinner and a movie, cautiously accept.
D. Be willing to become friends at work only because he is a co-worker and you are all too familiar with the pitfalls of dating in the workplace.

Answer: D. Ladies, are you familiar with the phrase "don't shit where you eat"? Men are. And believe me, we stick to this rule hard and fast. The last thing you want to do is become sexual with any co-worker. First, *all* and I do mean *all* of your dirty lingerie will be the hot topic at every cubicle on your floor. Second, you have exactly two chances of this progressing to a meaningful relationship: jack and shit. It's not gonna happen. Did you forget the rule? Don't shit where you eat. If a man is willing to jeopardize his work (meaning his money), it will be for something far greater than just a quick hit or a booty call, which is all you will ever be if you let things progress to a physical point. It doesn't matter how nice he is, how '"together" he is, what he looks like, or what he drives, the fact is, he does all these things while working with you! Not a good idea. Save yourself the embarrassment and headache, and let this one pass.

3. Ladies, you're in the midst of a wonderful first telephone conversation with a new male friend. You're relaxed on your couch, you're sipping on a glass of white zinfandel, *Sex and the City* is playing quietly in the background, and he actually has had some interesting things to say, thus far. You're doubly delighted, as his conversation is intellectual, and his voice is oh so sexy. You're starting to think good thoughts here. You ask

him one of our crucial questions: "Have you ever had any legal trouble?" There's a small pause ... a small sigh. He makes an effort to answer: "No, but there was this time when I had to stab this person ..." How do you respond, ladies? How do you respond?

A. You say, "Oh my goodness, you poor man. You must have been so frightened; tell me what happened."
B. You become excited and say, "Really? You know I have an ex-boyfriend who probably needs to be stabbed. Do you still do that type of stuff? We could go out after you take care of that ...my treat."
C. You become immediately turned off at even the hint of violence, because you know that at least 25 percent of the women (at least one out of every four) in America report being raped or physically assaulted by a current or former spouse, cohabitating partner, or date at some point in their lives, so you politely end the conversation.[6]
D. You say, "Whoo, I sure am tired. I didn't know it was this late ... 7:45 PM ... way past my bedtime. I have to be up tomorrow for cross-stitch quilting lessons at the local YMCA. Can't miss those. Bye-bye now." Abruptly hang up the phone, and hope to God you never mentioned anything to him about where you work or live or work out.

Answer. D or C. Actually, any form of rejection will work for this one. The actual sound you should have heard in your head was this: screech! Stop right there, ladies. At that point, you should have been standing, turning your TV off, downing your last few sips of wine, going into your bedroom, and going to sleep, as you should have brought this conversation to an immediate end. There is no acceptable explanation to "I had to stab this guy" that should suit you. If you're Puff Daddy and you're holding interviews for a new bodyguard, his answer about stabbing someone is not only acceptable but may also be a prerequisite for the position. However, you're not Puff Daddy, and you don't need security at a concert or nightclub; you just need security in your life and relationship—the kind that is usually not provided by strange men who stab people. End the conversation, and get a good nights rest. Tomorrow, the search continues. Sorry.

4. Okay, you finally agreed to go out for a first date with a gentleman you've recently been getting to know. You picked a quaint little tapas bar for light dinner and drinks. He's never heard of it. Even better—you can also show him something new for your first date. He shows up on time (first plus), smartly dressed (second plus), and in the same car he was driving when you met (wow, three pluses in a row!). Dinner is going well, and you are delighted by the conversation but are becoming somewhat annoyed by the unusually high number of male and female patrons and workers who come up and say hi to him throughout the course of the evening. He also seems to be getting an unusually high volume of calls and text messages on his cell phone as well. He says they are people he knows from "going out a lot in the past." You pay it no attention. You overhear a slim, swarthy-looking male ask your new friend if he's "partying tonight." He shakes his head no and says he doesn't party like that anymore. You notice a new look in his eyes: wide, a little glazed over, searching the room like he's excited about something. What might he be excited about, ladies? What could it be?

A. The extremely short micromini that keeps riding up your thighs and giving him sneak peeks of that ever-so-gorgeous expanse of skin and muscle you call a thigh.

B. The aggressively plunging neckline of that beautiful top you found especially for this date. He's complimented you on it all night and thinks to himself he even might have

seen a "nip slip" … oh, joy!
C. The possibility that he has finally found someone cool, beautiful, charming, and interesting, and that he may spend some time investing in getting to know you and possibly more.
D. The memory of the last time he "partied" with his friends and the exquisite, near blissful feelings he had that night, as they all seemed so friendly and loving. That's what is was … sort of like a love fest. And he's seriously considering ditching you and hanging with them tonight.

Answer: D. Okay, there are several clues here, if you're paying attention. First, you picked the place, yet he knows damn near everyone in there. Second, his friends are both male and female, all making similar comments. Third, he became quite distracted after the mention of partying later. Ladies, if you think you've never dated a man with a substance abuse problem, think again. You're on a date with one now! "Partying" is code for a cocaine party or an Ecstasy party. (Actually, it's code for whatever time and place you want to spend snorting, ingesting, inhaling, or shooting foreign substances into your body.) His inner cocaine beast was awoken tonight, and you, my dear, will be taking a backseat on this ride. My advice to you is to tell him to "please, spend time with your friends" and politely excuse yourself from the evening. Unless, of course, you fancy partying yourself. Then, by all means, party on, dudes! People with drug problems are initially very adept at hiding the fact that they have problems—they hide it from themselves and from others. They typically say things like "I used to have a problem with crack," or "I tried a lot of stuff when I was younger," or "I only use when I need to relax for a while." All of these comments are red flags that he is a once and future drug-addicted individual.

For those of you who haven't had the unique experience of being in a relationship with an addict, consider yourself lucky.

For those of you who have, tell the other half of the class to run, now! Addictive personalities are a lifelong issue. People who are addicted to substances have lifelong issues. Addiction can, and often does, drain mental, physical, family, and monetary resources. The truth of substance treatment is this: no one can make anyone stop using drugs except that person themselves. The addict has to connect his or her use with some loss or decline in function in certain areas of life and has to choose to change. Because it is just that—a choice. You can't do it for them. I can't do it for them. You and I can only provide the addict with tons of support once the individual decides that he or she wants help. Being in a relationship with someone who later develops a drug habit after you become a couple is an unfortunate circumstance, and obviously you do what you feel you must to help someone you care about. However, choosing to knowingly get involved with a person who you know or suspect has a drug habit is a foolish choice. Choose again. Move on.

DATING

Ah, the very mention of that vague and nebulous term gives guys great pleasure. It's so … poorly defined. We love it! It's one of those few words that can invoke two totally different emotions when mentioned. For guys, satisfaction. For women, frustration. If we're dating, you're more to me than just a booty call. However, less than a full-fledged girlfriend. But what are you, then? The truth is, it doesn't matter to me what you are because whatever it is, you are not my girlfriend. Ladies, guys would date you forever if you let us. The only reason we're even calling what we're doing "dating" is because you wanted to know "what are we?" or "where is this going?" So, we placate you with this term. It serves the purpose quite well for extended periods of time—time we may well use to find someone else (someone we think is hotter, smarter, or just all-around better) or to have sex with as many other women as we possibly can before you make us say we're now in a "committed relationship." Sorry, guys. I know this is a big secret to divulge. Think about it, ladies. You know I'm right. "Dating" means nothing. There is no commitment. There is no promise of monogamy. There is no guarantee that this will progress into something more (not even if you get pregnant). For guys, dating basically means we're hanging out, going out, and sometimes having sex. We enjoy the time we spend with you and are honestly enjoying becoming more comfortable around you. We're just not yet convinced that we always want to do these things with you and only you—yet.

What does dating mean to you, ladies? Think about it. You must be honest with yourself. This is a point in the relationship where, a lot of times, women get the lines blurred between what they want the relationship to be versus what the relationship actually is. Oftentimes, you will read more meaning into things that he may say or do because you want so badly for his words and actions to mean what you hope they might mean. I've seen this pattern continue until one day, reality stares you in the face, and you're forced to recognize that what you thought was happening was not. What you thought was a great relationship that was growing into something more meaningful was not. Some women have a tendency to react poorly at this time. Did he lie to you, or did you lie to yourself?

Disappointment. What you expected to happen didn't happen, and most, if not every time, that conversation after the letdown starts off with you saying something like "but you said we were dating." Exactly! But you heard what you wanted to hear. For guys, dating is a very concrete, non-fluid, non-progressive situation. The boundaries are well defined, and if at any time during the course of this dating interaction, those boundaries are crossed, we reserve the right to terminate this arrangement. That means no pop-up visits, no surprises, no standing Saturday night dates, and for damn sakes, no leaving any (I mean *any*) of your belongings at our place! Why? Because we're just dating. It's beautiful. This round of verbal jousting is one of the few times when a guy may actually get the last word with you. It is the be-all and end-all, the alpha and omega, our surgical strike, or as my brother the ex-Marine (which means he's still a Marine) would say: "the nipple of the tit."

Ladies, I need you to strip away from your mind all that you have come to believe about what dating means and see it for what is really is. If and when the day comes when you want more, perhaps more routine or monogamy, and you force us to make a decision at that relationship crossroads, then, and only then, will we define what exactly it is we're doing. That conversation usually starts off with you saying something to the effect of "I can't do this anymore," or "I need more," or "I don't even know what we are." If we like you and really are interested in being in a relationship with you, then and only then will we upgrade you to girlfriend status! If not, don't be surprised if and when we say something to the effect of "ending it altogether" or "we can just be friends" (but call you the next week to try to downgrade you to booty call status).

Interestingly enough, the lies that men tell during this time are few and far between. Here, we don't have to lie, because we don't have much to hide. I'm enjoying going out with you, I'm enjoying your company, I'm enjoying seeing you naked on occasion, and I'm really enjoying the whole nonexclusive thing. Again, we have precious little to hide here. If and when the time comes that you find out something morally questionable or downright offensive about us, we simply give you a moment to see whether or not you can handle the truth. If you can, it's cool, and things can continue as planned. If you can't, okay, then you'll hear that "I guess things just aren't working out for us" speech. In this situation, ladies, men are like Robert De Niro in the movie *Heat* (which is a damn fine crime drama that stars both him and Al Pacino, pitted against each other in the primes of their criminal and criminal catcher careers, by the way). Robert De Niro has a line that says there is nothing in his life he isn't prepared to "walk out on in thirty seconds flat if he spots the heat around the corner." The true test of the dating phase is when you ask us to "take it to the next level." If we are truly interested in pursuing something meaningful with you, we will agree and move the thing along to relationship/ girlfriend-boyfriend status. If we are not interested, you may hear lies like "I just have a lot going on right now," "I still don't

54

think I'm ready to be in a committed relationship," "I just want to be more stable for us first," "Don't you think we're moving a little too fast? Maybe we should slow down for a bit," or the all-time classic "I've been hurt before, so now I'm really careful with my heart." Ha! You gotta love that one! Guys like that last one almost as much as we love two-for-one dances at a strip club! Don't fall for it, ladies. All men are Robert De Niro at this point. Evaluating the situation, weighing the pros and cons, planning an exit strategy, and becoming prepared to walk away from you and never, ever look back.

No means no. I repeat: no means no, I don't care how nicely we say it or how gently we let you down. And honestly, some of the subterfuge here really is coming from a good place. We honestly don't want to hurt your feelings or disappoint you. But don't be fooled; most of it is coming from a place of selfishness, from the land of having our cake and eating it too. This is a critical point in the relationship, ladies. If you lose the dating battle at wounded heart, it will very likely deteriorate into something less, something only sexual, something only sporadic and unplanned, something with few if any intimate conversations, or something in which you don't even feel comfortable sharing personal things about yourself because you slowly realize that the two of you are no longer close. Then you move on. Or, if the battle goes well, that is to say, you have defined clearly what your expectations were, he has "taken some time to think about it" (by the way, any tough question you ask us, we always "take some time to think about it" … it's like a grace period for our more slowly performing brains), has thought about it, has thought about losing you and could not imagine that life, and has instead decided that he, too, would like to pursue a more meaningful relationship with you and only you. At this point, ladies, this is not a lie. This is honestly what he is thinking and truly what he means. Don't be distracted by that dragging sound you hear; it's just the sound of his feet dragging as he marches toward monogamy hill. It's a big deal for us guys, knowing that all couples activities we engage in will now include you, as you will be making up the other half of that couple.

The last thing guys do before we agree is to run a mental checklist of contacts, to try to assess just how much easy, free, silly, skanky, crazy, bonkers, hot, nasty, filthy, morally compromising sex partners we're gonna have to give up. And as we struggle to get that wistful smile off our faces, the more mature of us will come to realize that, in some cases, what we are gaining is so much more than what we would have to give up, that really it's an easy decision at this point. In some cases, here, ladies, we honestly believe we have found someone special and are interested in dating you and only you from this point on.

I'm a huge music lover and, as such, I have a song (or two) for every occasion. My song for the dating occasion is from the Spinners, entitled "That's the Way Love Goes." This classic song talks about a boy and a girl meeting, falling madly in love, and vowing to stay together. Then, as time passes, they grow older and leave each other. And that's the way love goes sometimes. It's a great song for whenever you're seeking clarity in relationships!

And that's the simple truth to dating. It is what it is. Something to be enjoyed. Something to appreciated. And—if it offers a promise of more—something to be explored. However, all dating relationships are not made to last. The wisdom here is in learning how to let go. Patients ask me "well, what's the point if it's just gonna end? Why do it at all?" I say, because we must. People need people. People need to feel love and share love and make love and be loved. And the truth is, even though a relationship ends, that doesn't mean it wasn't good for a time. It was not all bad. There were good times there, that no one will be able to take away from you. The good times were good, so hold on to that. Hold on to what you learned that was positive and true from it. Become aware of what wasn't good and how that started, so that you can better avoid making some of those same mistakes again. But don't ever ask what's the point, because there are no purely all bad or evil experiences in life (even though some of us guys may seem purely evil at times).

Pop Quiz:

1. Ladies, you're on a fabulous first date, with good food, good music, and freely flowing alcohol. You haven't had this much fun in a long time and haven't felt this comfortable around a man in an even longer time. He's driving you home in his nicely appointed Mercedes ('08, you think) and asks, "Are you ready for the night to end?" You say no and agree to head back to his place to watch a DVD and perhaps sip coffee (for those of you who don't know, that's dating code for "making out and perhaps having sex " ... I need for us to all be on the same page here). So you're back at his place, and it is *huge* ... (his place, I mean), nicely decorated, and it feels very homey, so you settle in, the make-out session ensues. During the make-out session, he keeps saying that he shouldn't because he has to be up early in the morning or he is kinda tired or he has a busy day tomorrow or really shouldn't be up this late. But curiously, he never puts the brakes on the making out part. (He's just priming the pump, ladies.) After the sex is over (you knew it was going there, right?), he immediately goes to the bathroom, tidies up a bit, and comes out dressed. He turns all of the once-dim mood lighting up ... and there's no cuddling. He asks you if you need anything in the bathroom while he goes to get some water (code for "get your ass dressed, so I can take you home immediately"). On the ride home, you are fairly silent. He asks what's on your mind. What do you say, ladies? What do you say?

A. Oh, nothing. I just want you to know I don't usually do that on a first date. (Yeah, yeah, ladies, we know ...

neither do we ... just tonight ... because you were ...
special ... and we felt a connection. Oh, the lies!)

B. I hope you don't think differently of me because I had
sex with you on the first date. (Actually, ladies, you just
confirmed exactly what we thought of you when we first
asked you out—fun, quick, and easy. Sorry.)

C. That was great; it had been awhile for me. I hope to see
you again, and we can continue to get to know each other
better and see where this relationship goes.

D. Is it too soon for me to tell you I love you? Because I
do, you know. Nobody has ever made me feel that way
before... you were amazing!

E. All of the above.

F. None of the above.

Answer: F. None of the above. I have news for you, ladies.
You just became a booty call! It doesn't matter what you say at
this point. You could say you're the new and future Queen of
England with a dowry the size of the Federal Reserve Bank,
and it won't change the fact that the next time we see you, it will
be late, quick, sexual, and you will be going home immediately
after we're done. Booty call! It is what it is. He set it up perfectly
throughout the course of the evening, and you fell right in line.
Now I realize that for some of you, a booty call isn't necessarily
a bad thing, as that may be all you are interested in as well. If
that's the case, then proceed. However, if that is not all you
want out of this relationship, it will be exceedingly difficult
from here to have us see you as anything other than that, and
you may want to put a limit on the amount of times you allow
us to call on you for such evening duties. Look alive here, ladies.
Getting caught up in that first booty call session is kind of like a
car accident. It all happens so fast that you never see it coming,
and in the end, nobody is really sure whose fault it was.

2. Ladies, your cell phone rings. It's your girlfriend calling.

She says, "Girl, doesn't your man drive a new black convertible Mercedes? I think I just saw him going into the movies with somebody!" What do you do, ladies? What do you do?

A. Get the location of the movie theater, drive there, and wait in the parking lot by his car to see "exactly what the hell is going on."
B. Have your girlfriend check the tag number (because, of course, you have his license plate number memorized) to simply verify if it is him or not.
C. Begin crying hysterically, and ask your girl to come over and talk to you about him, because you "knew something was going on."
D. Dismiss that lying, conniving, manipulative girlfriend's comment as an attempt to cause confusion between you and your man because, deep down, you know she does not want you to be with him anyway (not because anything's wrong with him, mind you … nothing other than the fact that he's with you and not her).

Answer: D. Again ladies, it's a trick question. The answer is in the question. He's a viable, heterosexual male with means and perhaps good taste! You know damn well that one, if not all, of your girlfriends have had eyes for him the minute you introduced them … come on … get real. Search your feelings. You'll find it to be true. It's happened time and time again and will continue to happen until you open your eyes to the reality of the situation. The two of you are just dating. Which means you're not married. Which means to other single ladies that he's pretty much available! Your girlfriends are no exception. You know what they say: a good man is hard to find. Lucky for your girlfriend, you found one for her! You have to see this type of manipulation coming, and keep your man and your girlfriends on separate islands. You don't need to be the captain of the ferryboat between them.

3. You've been dating this really great guy for about six months now. The conversation is never stale, the sex is great, and he can even cook (bonus!). You've met a fair amount of his friends, but curiously you don't know much about and have never laid eyes on anyone in his family. He'll be out of town next weekend to attend his sister's wedding. He hasn't officially invited you yet, but you believe it's just an oversight, because he's been so busy with work lately, and it probably slipped his mind. As the day of the wedding approaches, ladies, you …

A. Clear your schedule and buy a cute and tasteful dress to wear for the first time you meet his parents and family. (Yaay! It's so exciting.)

B. Become somewhat concerned that he hasn't invited you yet, as the day approaches, but nevertheless plan on attending, because surely he wouldn't dare go home for such a big event as this and not take the woman he's dating.

C. Become urgently panicked because he has not uttered a word about you going with him yet. You call an urgent girlfriend high counsel meeting into session and discuss just what he might be thinking. (Did he just forget? Is he assuming that you know you'll be going? Is there someone else he might be taking? Is there an old flame at home he doesn't want you to meet? Maybe he's ashamed of his family? Maybe his "sister" isn't really his sister at all but is in fact his uncle, who's fresh home from a Third World prison and recovering from a "gender altering" surgery. Umm, sorry. Too far out there? Okay.)

D. Do not get the least bit upset if he does or does not invite you home for the wedding, because you understand that you and he are "just dating."

Answer: D. (Was there any doubt?) Of course, ladies! Do not be fooled, whether it's three months or three years—if we're just dating, we are under no obligation to have you meet any of our closest friends and surely not anyone in our family. That is a privilege reserved specifically for a girlfriend, which you are not, because you are just "the girl I'm dating." Beautiful in its vague simplicity! Just remember, ladies: unless you have specifically had the "take this to the next level" talk and have come to a mutual agreement on what the next level is and have actually heard the words "yes, we can" come from his mouth, then do not assume that girlfriend status has been obtained.

To Commit or Not to Commit

Ahhh, "Committed Relationship Way." What a great road to drive on a lazy Sunday. Guys learn about things here on this scenic route that were previously foreign to us. We learn about Sunday brunches, white sales, your real dress and shoe sizes, crumb trays, at last, at long last, we learn exactly how to fold a fitted sheet! Being in a committed relationship definitely has its pluses. There is something to be said for knowing what you have. Knowing that you have someone to regularly do things with. Knowing that you have someone to share meaningful things and events and milestones in your life with. Knowing you have someone who is genuinely interested in you and in whom you are genuinely interested as well. Knowing you have someone to count on. It's stability. It's comfort. It's the natural progression in the relationships of mature individuals. Mature individuals being the operative word here.

Unfortunately, ladies, a lot of you have been dating guys with backstage passes to the "mental midget extravaganza" (sorry; technically, they're "little people")! All those things that are good and decent about being in a loving, committed relationship, these men do not value. Those things are what *you* value and think about relationships, but most of these guys think differently. What they're thinking about is all the things they are going to have to give up: Free time, Clint Eastwood movies on AMC on Sunday afternoon, free time, nights out with the boys, free time, time spent in pursuing women who have no interest in them, free time, gym time spent working on that ever-evolving spare tire, free time, watching the ball game while eating leftover pizza (it's a guy thing), free time, free time, and free time! There is nothing you can do to change this. There is nothing you can say to change this. There is no amount of quality time you can spend with him to change this. It's a maturity issue. His—not yours. It is something that men must realize, become troubled by, and then want to change. Ladies, you cannot do this for them! You cannot change our minds for us!

If you have a man who enjoys all there is to offer from a committed relationship, ladies, congratulations! You hit the relationship lottery! However, if you happen to be one of those ladies whose beau has not yet learned to appreciate the journey of being on the road to commitment, then strap your boots on, ladies; shit is about to get deep.

The lies men tell here are lies for an exodus. We are trying to escape! We just want to get away for a while, just a little while, just a quick minute, just for the briefest of seconds, to catch our breath, clear our heads, get our bearings, and get back to ourselves. Whew! We will make up some of the most ridiculous of excuses to spend some time away from you; stop me if you've heard these before. "Need to run to the car parts store real quick." "Gonna run to the gas station real quick." "Gonna run to Steve's house real quick." "Gonna hit the gym real quick." "Gotta go back in to work real quick." And my all-time favorite vague excuse to get away from you: "Gotta make a run real quick." Everything initially starts off as "real quick" because it's just that. We need a quick breather. We don't plan on being gone long, just long enough.

Ladies, we're drowning. And like all drowning men on the brink of death, we yearn for just a quick chance to come up for air. Just a glimpse of that pretty blue sky again. Just a quick burst of fresh air, so our lungs can remember what it feels like to breathe again. Let us have it, ladies; it's a small price to pay for a man who comes back home actually glad to see you. A quick breather here can save a life—the life of your relationship. Oh, and by the way, the last thing that men want to hear on their way out the door is "Well, how long will you be gone?". Damn! Don't remind us! Just let us go. The easier the way out, the quicker we will come back. It's that pressure thing rearing its ugly head again. If you haven't figured it out yet, most guys don't respond well to pressure. We don't like it. Take the pressure off, and we will come through and perform beautifully. Keep the pressure on, and we will show you just what a big disappointment we can be. It's ass-backward, I know, but some of you have seen this phenomenon for yourselves by now, I'm sure.

And where we go is really irrelevant. Hell, most times we don't even know where we're going. We just get in the car and drive for a little while. It's that feeling of being unshackled that we seek; where we find it is of no consequence. Fear not, ladies. The lies here initially are not covering up any unscrupulous behavior. It is what it is. We just want a little break. And the minute you give men (like all children) what it is they think they want, then they don't want it anymore. Oftentimes, they will even call you while they're out, because they honestly miss you. Crazy, right? I know. We don't understand it either. What you have to understand, ladies, is that a man reaching the point where he is grateful for what he has in a relationship is a process of growth. He must be allowed the time and space for that journey. And just like most things that grow, it's not something men are continually doing. Oftentimes growth happens in spurts. And in between those spurts, breaks must occur. Taking breaks is an important part of a man's relationship growth, for him to eventually get to a point where he is able to appreciate what you offer. It's the natural ebb and flow. It's the yin and the yang. It's the perfect belt and shoes to complement your purse! All these things must be allowed, or else it throws the whole thing off.

Here's a hypothetical situation for you to ponder. We have a woman, stunningly gorgeous! Men who meet her say she is the most singularly beautiful woman they've ever known. The most curious thing about her is that her beauty seems to spring from the inside. She has a heart the size of Texas! Perhaps you know someone like her. At any rate, when she meets a new guy friend, because she is very cautious, she asks tons of very specific questions. I mean, tons! She demands honesty. She demands sincerity, and her rules are simple. She will get to know you, date you, and enjoy spending time with you, but you will not see her naked unless there is a commitment. It's her "no commitment-no naked" rule. Nothing wrong with that, right? She probably does it the way it should be done—actually getting to know someone first. However, she has had something other than success with guys she's chosen in the past. Most of her former beaus have had a taste for lying. Not just little white lies, but huge "whale of a lie" lies! So what happens? What goes wrong? What is she doing wrong? Well, let's look at it.

First, let's look at her. She's stunningly beautiful. Most men react unpredictably when confronted with a woman of that physicality. Either we see her, we want her, and will do anything to possess her (including but not limited to lying), or we see her, want her, become scared shitless of the idea of having her, run a list of why she wouldn't want to be with us, and then run away. It's cliché, but it's true. The other thing that happens with her is the commitment issue. She makes it very clear that it will not become sexual if he has other partners. Force a man's hand, why don't you? Seriously, that's like locking a five-year-old kids in a candy store for the weekend and telling them they can have any piece of candy they want, but once they pick it, they have to eat only that kind of candy for the whole weekend and no other candy! Good luck! No way in hell that

that any child could follow those instructions—same with men when dating this woman. The thing that happens here is kind of ironic. She is such the total package, beauty, brains, family-oriented, and devoted, that it's kind of like a no-brainer with guys. We meet someone like her, get to know her, and have no doubt that she'd make a fabulous wife whenever we're ready. But for us to be ready is part of the problem.

In this scenario, it's not the woman's fault. The men in her life just aren't ready. Not ready for someone like her and someone as real as her. As men, when we find someone like this, but we know we're not ready for something this real, we will do something very curious. Obviously, we don't want her to get away, but we can't quite make that leap to total commitment just yet, so we will attempt to hold on to her while we try to rid ourselves of the TGV (Trashy Girl Virus). Oh, what a terrible affliction this is! It's laid waste to many a town and to many a man and his family. Unfortunately, there's only one way to cure a virus, and that is to let it run its course. Which means that men have to go through a certain number of trashy girls before they can truly appreciate and be ready for someone wholly beautiful.

So, with the lady in this scenario, the men attempt to rid themselves of the TGV while they hold onto her, and the inevitable happens. She finds out. Things end poorly. My fear is that she will let these immature guys steal her most prized possession: her loving heart. I hope she can hold on until her knight in shining armor comes to rescue her, as she is truly a princess, as many of you reading this book are, as well! Don't let the peasants of the world ruin you, ladies! Your knight is out there, and he'll cross that drawbridge to your castle when the time is right. Be patient and wise, and for God sakes, don't let the little boys eat all of your candy!

As your committed relationship gains momentum, the reason for the lies will change. At some point in this thing, all men are gonna ask themselves the same questions: "Is this it?" "Are you it?" "Are you the one?" "Is this the woman I'm gonna spend the rest of my life with?" "Is this the woman who I'm gonna raise kids with?" "Is this honestly the last woman I'm ever gonna see naked in person?" (Thank God for the instant porn box some people curiously refer to as a computer.) It is at this time when the lies have the potential to grow into something more ... sinister. Men are all scientists at heart. We come up with a hypothesis, develop it into a theory, and then, of course, we have to test it. If the theory is "this is it," then, of course, we have to know for sure. Here, ladies, is where we will undertake frantic desperate measures to "make sure" you are the one.

The excuses to get away will become more elaborate. The time spent away will become more extended. That wistful, forlorn look we sometimes have will become a look of downright detachment. Some guys become outright cranky for no apparent reason, almost like we're looking to start a fight. (Actually, we are, so we can become angered and storm out ... *out* being the operative word and ultimate goal.) Ladies, we'll begin to test the limits of your patience and intelligence. Be concerned; be very concerned. This is a time that must be handled with tact and kid gloves (mostly because you're dealing with a child).

Men here will test limits and boundaries. just like they did when they were children, only with different stakes on the line. We are going to start hanging out with the boys more, just to make sure we're not missing out on anything. We may get really serious about our jobs all of a sudden, trying to assess just how far we can go there. And, yes, ladies, we will definitely attempt (sometimes rather clumsily) to spend time with other women. Gasp! It's no big deal (for us anyway). It's just to see, just for funsies; we just have to know if you are truly the one. Fear not; that time spent with other women doesn't necessarily mean that we're having sex with them. We just "wanna see." I know, I know ... you may ask what we wanna see. That's just it. We don't know, exactly. We just have to see. We want to see if there's anyone else out there we think we might get along with better. We want to see if there's anyone else out there we think we may have better chemistry with. We want to see if there's anyone else out there we think we may enjoy having sex with more than you. We want to see if there's anyone else out there who might care about us more, be nicer to us, complement us better, or make us feel better about who we think we are. All these things we must "see." It's frustrating, I know, ladies, but I ask you to bear with us here.

If there is a mustard seed–sized grain of maturity in him, he will soon see what you already know: that you indeed are the one and, yes, this is it. The truth here, ladies, is that no matter how many excuses we give you to get out of the house, no matter how many times we go out with the boys, no matter how many questionable "business lunches" or "business trips" we take, we learn very quickly that that bucket-o'-lies is quite empty. The time spent in pursuing these fishing expeditions usually is just wasted time. We do it because we think we must, but the truth is, it's not very enjoyable. The truth is, we spend most of that time thinking about you! (Damn you for that …)

Ladies, the key here for you is patience. You have to handle us no differently than you would a toddler approaching the terrible twos and testing limits or an unruly teenager with raging hormones rebelling against the rules. Try to predict the things your man may say and do at this time and figure out why (just as you would with a child). And, as with kids or teens, you can't stop it altogether, but you can hope to contain it to just a few rooms in the house. All of you moms out there know what I'm talking about. Ladies without children, ask your mothers or parental figures in your life, and they will explain that one to you.

And you must be able to keep your emotions to a controllable level. That is critical to your success. Actually, any increased emotion from you here is just another excuse for us to get away from you, take a break, and blow off some steam. Make no mistake, you are in a battle, and guys are not going to fight fair. You're fighting for the preservation of a current and future democratic society. He's a rebel militiaman trying to topple and overthrow your strange ways of life. Emotion here is your enemy. High emotion here is our "aha" moment. We say, "Aha, I knew it! I knew you couldn't handle it!" And we may ride that aha right out of the relationship (or at least to the corner store). Keep a level head. This, too, shall pass. I think that subconsciously, men are trying to elicit from you ladies the same increased amount of high emotion and anxiety we're actually feeling on the inside to validate our own feelings. So, in part, ladies, showing that emotion is a good thing. However, consciously men will make an effort to use that emotion against you. It's a bit of a catch-22 for women. High emotion is the only part of this situation that makes sense for us. It's the only familiar element to us at this time, as we venture into what is, for most guys, new territory, where we're finally having real emotions with real consequences. What we do at this moment affects the rest of our lives. For better or for worse!

The other subconscious feeling that we have, that can manifest in a relationship at this time, is insecurity. If she is the one, "the woman," then does that mean I'm (gulp) "the man"? Does that mean I'm gonna have to do all those things that real men do, like get up and go to work every day? Every day. Come home at the end of every day? Every day. Be able to provide for us ... (geesh ... us)? Think about planning for our future? Then actually plan for the future? Be responsible? Be accountable? Be transparent, or that is to say, be very willing to speak what I am thinking and feeling so as not to make her have to figure out where I'm coming from? This is a crucial skill to master.

Now is the time to consider all these changes, because from here is where you begin to build foundations for what comes next in the natural progression of relationships. I keep saying natural progression, because it should be just that—natural. It should not feel like you're trying hard, and it should not feel like you're making an effort. It should not feel like work at this point. Now we know that any solid relationship gets there by both people working at it. But it shouldn't feel like work. It should feel natural, just doing and saying the things that come naturally to us as we begin to learn more about each other and begin to care more about each other and as we begin to fall in love with each other. If you or I feel like we have to clock in every day in our relationship, then one day, one of us might clock out and not come back.

Pop Quiz:
1. You're having a delicious dinner with your man at your favorite restaurant. The mood is right, the music is right, the lighting is highlighting that new thing you're doing with your eye shadow perfectly, and you're in a deep, meaningful discussion about what it would be like to be married to each other. All of a sudden, out of the blue, almost on cue, he seems very distracted. He is unable to keep his gaze off of the table directly behind you. You quickly turn around and see the unthinkable! You see what has to be probably the two most gorgeous women you (and surely he) have ever seen, with bright young faces sitting atop long, graceful necklines plunging to curiously full spherical objects seemingly floating in their own orbits! Oh my God, could it be? Yes, they are the fabled "smokin' hot" women, right behind you! Carrying on what seems to be just a delightful light conversation among themselves. What do you do, ladies? What do you do?

A. Become incensed and irate and launch into a tirade about his immaturity and wandering eyes.
B. Become incensed and irate and launch into a tirade about his immaturity and wandering eyes and then throw your drink in his face right before you storm out of the restaurant.
C. Become so frustrated and disappointed in him that you

simply remain silent for the rest of the evening.

D. Realize that this must be that "acting out" behavior Dr. Major told you about and simply ignore it, because you realize that just like with a child, the way to extinguish a behavior you don't want is by not rewarding it with any attention.

Answer: D. Yaay! Now you're getting it! The truth is that it doesn't matter what those women at the next table look like or what they are doing. They could look like last week's trash that blew off the truck! It's not about what or who they are. It's about what they represent: a distraction. A distraction from what was becoming an uncomfortable conversation for your man, and so he did what all good pitchers do, who are trying to control and win a ball game: he threw you a curveball. Your job is not to fall for it ... don't swing!

2. You and your man have just finished a delicious meal at your favorite restaurant. You're feeling tipsy and in the mood for a very romantic finish to the night. He pays for the meal, and you notice he leaves an eight-dollar tip in the form of four two-dollar bills. You say, "Gee, I haven't seen one of those in a while. Where did you get them?". He says, "Uh, oh, that's all they had for change when I went to the car wash the other day." What do you suspect, ladies?

A. Suspect nothing, as car washes are notorious for handling different forms of American currency, specifically two-dollar bills.
B. Suspect nothing, as you are stuffed, tipsy, and horny and want to head home for the "big finish."
C. Suspect he probably got them from gambling with the boys again at poker night, and become concerned because you don't want his gambling to become an issue for you later, once you're married and have such responsibilities

like mortgages and the kids' college funds.

D. Suspect nothing, because there is no need to suspect, because you already know! You know damn well for a fact that the one and only place he would have gotten two-dollar bills is at the local strip club—the same strip club you specifically voiced your disdain of and forbade him to enter!

Answer: D. They're called strip clubs, ladies. Places with free-flowing alcohol and strange, new half-naked women in clear heels vying for our attention. (Some guys call it heaven.) We like them, so deal with it. Remember that night we had to "make a run real quick," well, this is where we went.

3. You are seeing a fabulous guy and have been in a committed relationship for the better part of the last year. You have even allowed yourself to imagine the occasional wedding bell or two. You've hit the jackpot; he's loving, caring, open, honest, and seemingly has little to hide from you. One Sunday morning while he goes out for coffee and you are left at his place tallying up your monthly bills, you mistakenly open his cellular phone bill statement, because you thought it was yours. (Damn that "favorite five"!) You are shocked and dismayed to find that there are several lengthy calls at late hours to a 704 area code (isn't that Atlanta, where he just moved from?). As you read on (you've invaded his privacy this far, so there's no need to turn back now), you find a disturbingly high number of text messages to the same number, sent and received at very late hours. He comes back home with coffee and breakfast just as you finish resealing the envelope to his once-private statement. What do you do next, ladies? What do you do?

A. Confront that lying bastard immediately! How could he do this to you? You storm out of the house but not before you douse his Berber carpet with that coffee and tell him to take that breakfast and send it to "that bitch" he's been calling in Atlanta!

B. Become visibly upset but regain your composure as you begin to slowly and methodically cross-examine him about his telephone habits, just waiting for him to say something that contradicts what you have already found to be true, so you can catch that lying bastard in his own web of lies.

C. Calmly apologize to him for mistakenly opening his mail and violating his privacy and, more calmly still, ask him if there is anything you and he need to talk about, as you noticed there has been some questionable activity on his statement. You again apologize for the way you found out, but nonetheless, this is a committed relationship, and clearly this is a matter that must be dealt with.

D. Say nothing. Wait. Just wait. Because you know that if he cares for you like you think he does, this just may be one of those acting-out incidents that Dr. Major talked about men doing as they get closer to approaching the ultimate commitment in a relationship. Also, you believe in your heart of hearts that if, in fact, there is something going on, he will eventually not be able to hide it, and there will be clear and convincing evidence of his wrongdoing. Then, you will deal with it appropriately at that time. Until then, you will continue to look upon him with trusting eyes, albeit a bit more closely.

Answer: C. (A lot of you thought D, right?) I think there has been enough dishonesty here already. No need for you to add to it. You're both adults, and there is no need for you not to talk about the elephant in the room. You made a mistake by opening his mail. Own up to it. Hopefully, he will be adult enough to admit his mistake as well. If he reacts with hostility and indignation, sorry, ladies, but he's probably hiding something. If he reacts calmly and openly and doesn't seem to be scrambling for words and admits it was wrong to have that kind of contact with others outside of your relationship, then great! This just may serve as the model for how to calmly and openly discuss (that means converse, not yell at each other) all future concerns, disagreements, and issues that will undoubtedly crop up in your relationship.

TOUGH QUESTIONS ... HARD ANSWERS

In this chapter, I'll go through a host of questions that women typically ask in relationships—questions that most, if not all, men are deathly afraid of and often react to in the most unpredictable of ways. Once and for all, I'm going to give you ladies the brutal and honest truth. By brutal, I do not intend to be mean or cruel, just totally honest. Please don't take offense, and if you do take offense, then you might want to consider not asking these types of questions. We all have heard them, ladies; you know we hate them, and yet you still persist in asking them.

Question: *What are you thinking right now?*
White lie: Oh, nothing.
Honest answer: Obviously not about you. (As if the faraway look in our eyes and blank stare on our faces weren't enough to clue you in, our unusually still and distant body language should definitely make you aware. It could be anything, honestly. We could be thinking about our jobs, someone in our families, what we have to do next week, when our next vacation will be, if we're gonna wash the car today, what we want to eat for dinner, if there's anything good on TV, etc., etc. More than likely, we're actually thinking about that game or car show or Ultimate

Fighting Championship fight or ESPN-related broadcast that we've been staring at for the last ten minutes on TV. Honestly, ladies, when we say "nothing," it usually is just that. You'd be amazed how highly skilled most men are at wiping their minds totally blank for long periods of time. Rarely is it something as sinister as us thinking about having hot, nasty, filthy, morally compromising sex regularly with, and eventually dumping you for, that uncommonly beautiful, painfully funny, joy to be around, wish she could meet my momma, perfect example of a woman you curiously and routinely refer to as "my best friend, Jamie.")

Better yet: Rather than asking him what he's thinking about right now, feel free to just let him know straight-out what you're thinking about.

Question: *Do these jeans make my ass look fat?*
White lie: No, they look fine.
Honest answer: No, sweetie. (I use a term of affection here to soften the blow). I don't think it's the jeans that make your ass look fat; I think it may have more to do with the actual ass itself and not so much the jeans. Maybe a more flattering cut for you body style would look better. (You know damn well what the truth is, yet you still ask, just to get our take on the situation, to see our reaction. Why? There is no answer to this question that will be good enough for you, ladies. Why? Because it's a question born from insecurity on your part, and no answer we give you will be able to change what you think about yourself. It seems like any answer to this question undoubtedly leads to an argument or spat or tiff. Ladies, for our sake, please don't ask! We're here with you, so we honestly think it looks fine.)

Better yet: If you think you look fat in those jeans, change into something you feel good in. Then you won't even need to ask if you look fat, because you'll know you don't.

Question: *Do you think my friend Jamie is hot?* (Read "prettier than I am." Guys, please refer to description of "my best friend, Jamie" from the question above.)

White lie: No, I guess she's all right. I never really paid attention.

Honest answer: Yes. Yes, she is. In ye ol' Mexico, they call her *Infeugo*. You know it, I know it, blind men on Mars know it, and anyone who's ever seen her knows it. Why do this to yourself? The truth here is that it doesn't matter if she is or isn't, because I'm here with you. I'm in a relationship with you. Only you. I'm with you, because I want to be with you and no one else. If I wanted to be with someone else, I would break up with you and go try and be with that other person. (Ladies, please stop bringing unwanted guests into what should be our relationship. If you keep wanting us to compare and contrast you with other ladies, eventually we're gonna find a match-up that's not favorable for you.)

Better yet: If you think she's pretty, just say so. As a mature, secure couple, you both should be able to recognize and compliment attractive people of the opposite sex. Recognizing that in others in no way diminishes your attractiveness to each other. In fact, it only makes you more attractive because we can see your self-confidence, and self-confidence is probably the single most attractive trait of a woman to men.

Question: *What are you looking at?*

White lie: Nothing.

Honest answer: Oh, just that ungodly hot, young, carefree tart who probably enjoys hours on end of hot, nasty, filthy, morally compromising sex with zero commitment who's (I think she is not wearing a bra … gulp) walking this way. (Ladies, you know damn well what we are looking at, because you're looking at her too. Matter of fact, you saw her thirty seconds before we did and were just waiting to see how we would react when we finally did cast our eyes her way. Please don't ask. Let's just move on and go buy that down comforter that you say, and I guess I believe, we so desperately need for the bedroom.)

Better yet: Acknowledge the obvious, so we can move on. It's okay to talk about the elephant in the room or the "tart in tights," as it were. Again, complimenting another woman's beauty in no way diminishes your own beauty to us.

Question: *Do you love me?*

White lie: Of course, babe.

Honest answer: Yes. (Unfortunately, ladies, guys don't often say it and do even less to show it outright. From the man's mind, the thought process is this: I'm here with you, spending time in a relationship with you, so that should be enough to show that I do love you. We forget that sometimes it takes more than just being there to make a woman feel and know she is loved. The truth is, this question is a necessary evil for guys. We have to be asked, to remind us that we need to show our love more often.)

Better yet: Point out to us some little thing we did, and let us know how much it meant to you and how it made you feel loved. We will be more inclined to continue to do those types of things and to verbalize our feelings as well. Deep down, all men still have that little boy in them who desperately seeks acknowledgment and approval from the most important woman in their lives. Now that woman is you!

Question: *What do you like about me?*

White lie: Everything, especially your_____. (Fill in the blank with whatever it is we think you like most about yourself.)

Honest answer: Obviously, it depends on who you are, ladies. The answer here is going to be as unique and individualized as each of you. The tricky part here is not to take offense to what he doesn't say he likes about you. Don't be disappointed in thinking that a part of you that you really value he does not.

For guys, it's one of those "brain freeze" questions. What I hope, ladies, is that you are asking this question for genuine reasons and not because of some hidden insecurities that have you wondering just why we are with you. Be careful of your own intentions here.

Better yet: Ladies, help us focus our thoughts here. Point out something about yourself that you may be feeling unsure of, and ask us our honest opinion. That will open the door for an honest and open discussion, and we will then feel more comfortable pointing out to you the things we really like about you, because we would then be able to pick up on your train of thought and not view the question as a trap. Another good way to start this discussion is to ask us "what do you like about spending time with me?"

Question: *Why are you with me?*
White lie: Because you're you, babe.
Honest answer: See above question. This is a more direct path to the essence of the question above. Again, I'm not sure if this question needs to be answered. As people who have come to know themselves, we should know what we love and value about ourselves and should obviously expect the person we're with to love and value those same things. Certain truths don't bear reminders. Know and be confident in who you are and what dishes you bring to the relationship banquet, and trust that your partner will appreciate what you bring and present his own dishes to complement yours.

Better yet: Tell us why *you're* with *us.* You may be amazed at the barrage of insightful things your man will say about you in return!

Question: *Does my hair look all right?*
White lie: Yes.
Honest answer: Yes! (Guys, ladies … it's just not worth it to be honest in this case. "Yes" is the one and only answer to this

question. Guys, I don't care if her hair looks like she just got off of the whirling dervish at the super-duper, new and improved Walt Disney World—the answer is still yes. Specifically, "Yes, baby, your hair looks great." We might even throw in an "as usual" for good measure. This is a little white lie that is usually appreciated by both men and women. It goes a long way toward keeping the peace in an otherwise awkward dating moment.) There is no real "honest answer" in this situation because anything other than "yes" will likely be perceived as a criticism. A criticism of her hair? Yes. A criticism of her as a person? Perhaps. For men, it's hard to know just how a woman will respond to this answer. Her "hair" may be a subconscious metaphor meaning "do I look all right?" or "do I look all right enough to be with you?" or "am I good enough to be with you?" So, guys, unless you're ready to embark on what could quickly become a deep discussion about "why the two of you make a good match," then by all means … just answer yes!

Better yet: Say "I know it's not perfect right now, but I just want to make sure it's okay when I'm with you." (Ladies, you will be astounded at the newfound patience and tolerance men will find in this instance, because now we understand that the way your hair looks is more about securing us and not about insecure you!)

Question: *I just got my hair cut; do you like it?*

White lie: Yes, I love it.

Honest answer: I didn't know you needed it cut and can't really tell any difference. (But again, a little white lie here is forgivable.) Guys, say "yes, baby, I love it." If you get brave, you can even say "it really frames your face well." (Careful now; the savvy woman is gonna ask, "well, what kind of face do you think I have? Are you saying it's too round or too long?" Or whatever a guy could say here that's gonna cause an argument. Stick to your guns, cowboy. Simplicity is the key.) Say "just pretty, babe; you just have a pretty face." (Then, if allowed, immediately exit the room. In the olden days, men used to call this running for cover.)

Better yet: You can say "I just got my hair cut, but I'm not too sure about [whatever aspect of it]," and then ask our honest opinion. (Ladies, what guys need here is for you to give us direction and help focus our thoughts. If we can zero in on a particular aspect of the hair, it will better allow us to give you meaningful feedback. The truth is that most men have no idea how a woman's hair gets to look the way it does and are simply astounded at the creative visionaries who think up these different hairstyles, imagining that they will look cute. This is truly foreign soil for us, ladies, so please act as a guide.)

Question: *How many girlfriends have you had?*

White lie: Oh, not too many.

Honest answer: Define girlfriend. (Trust me, ladies, you've never known nausea until you've felt the nausea induced by hearing the honest answer to this question—until you hear the staggering number! Interestingly enough, this question is easier for guys to answer than for females. It's forgivable and, on some level, even attractive for a guy to have "been around the block" a few times. It's a double standard, I know. So typically. most guys don't have to scale down the number much. We just divide by two, subtract ten, and don't count anyone we've dated past the age of twenty-seven, because technically, she's more of a woman friend or a lady friend, not a "girl" friend. At any rate, you will never get the true whole number here, and truthfully you don't really want it. Why don't you ask the question you're really interested in? See below.

Better yet: If you are interested in his past levels of commitment, then you can ask what is the longest relationship he's ever been in. If you want to know the number of past sexual partners he's had, then ask him that (see below).

Question: *How many women have you had sex with?*

White lie: Not a lot.

Honest answer: Enough. Even if I could remember all of the names and all of the faces and all of the places of all the girls I've "loved" before, I actually cannot manipulate that type of higher math in my head. I'd need some scratch paper and a good calculator. (Again, ladies, you will never, ever, never, ever get that actual number.) I'm going to really stick to my "guy guns" here and say "however many I have slept with, it was enough to make me realize what I have in you that's so special." (Awwwww. Sappy, but true. I think, as long as he was careful, does not have any lingering lifelong effects from his previous partners, as in diseases or stray children, and is not currently sleeping with any of them, then the real number is not terribly important. We'll give you a general ballpark figure and try our best to change the subject.)

Better yet: You can tell us if you're feeling uncomfortable with what may be our different levels of sexual experience. Most men are fairly understanding about this and won't try to play Tarzan, king of the jungle, as they commence to "rock your everloving world." Instead, most men rather enjoy exposing you to new things and ideas in that arena. But be careful, ladies. Some men will surprise you with a very low number here—a number so low that your actual number of sexual partners dwarfs his in comparison. Your actual number plays "Gigantor" to his "Ant-Man." Your actual number is a blue whale to his minnow. Your actual number ... well, you get the picture. At any rate, be prepared, because this is a question that could backfire on you in a big way, and it's very hard for both sexes to hide the truth in their immediate reactions to this question.

Question: *Do you like fake boobs? I think they're funny-looking.*

White lie: No, I hate them too.

Honest answer: I only like them Monday through Friday; on weekends, I actually love them! I love them on a train. I love them on a plane. I love them in a car. I love them at a bar.

I also love Dr. Seuss. (Ladies, men love things with a plastic quality. I think it has something to do with the texture and the toylike nature of them. Same reason we love gadgets. Toylike. When we were boys, we liked toy cars and toy guns. Most of us still like toy cars and toy guns. Think about it: every guy you know has some sort of toy he still enjoys playing with to this day. Fake boobs are no exception—as well they should not be! It is what it is.)

Better yet: You can tell us if there is a part of your body that you feel you could improve and ask us about our opinion of women who get plastic surgery in general. I have found that what women are more concerned with here is how the men in their lives will perceive them if they have had work done. Will we think you're too superficial? Will we think there is a fake quality about you? Will we think you're overly concerned with your physical appearance? Will we think you're doing it to attract other men? Again, I think the better question is to ask him how he feels about women who have had any type of plastic surgery.

Question: *Did you sleep with her?*

White lie: No.

Honest answer: No, I did not sleep with her. She was not asleep, and neither was I. We were both wide-awake and quite alert the whole time. The sleepy part didn't come until after … so, no, sweetie, I did not sleep with her! (Ladies, if you have to ask, then you probably already know the answer. Sorry. It wasn't me; it was the TGV flaring up again.)

Better yet: If this is a question you need to ask, then this is a difficult time in your relationship. I don't think that *what* he did with her is as important as the *how* or *why*. What you really need to know here, ladies, is how and why those boundaries were broken and those lines were crossed, so you can gauge the chances of that happening in the future and what you will need to do to move on, if necessary.

Pop Quiz:

1. Ladies, you and your man are enjoying a wonderful day at the beach. The weather's great, the breeze is just right, and you're feeling quite fit, with the results you've gotten from your new Pilates classes. All of a sudden, it happens. The unthinkable! Her! She! That! The waters part, the clouds clear—hell, even the sea gulls stop singing—and there she stands, in all her toned, taut, and tanned glory. What you can only assume is that this is what a sea maiden or beach goddess must look like! What do you do, ladies? What do you do?

A. Recoil in anguish and insecurity as you brace for not only your man but all men in the immediate surrounding area to take note and fawn, swoon, drool, and otherwise embarrass themselves over this mermaid come-to-life?

B. Begin to feel bad about yourself as you compare yourself to her physically and allow this to absolutely ruin your day. Immediately begin to pack your things and proclaim to your man "I'm ready to go!"

C. Walk up to her and compliment her on her physical splendor and incredible "assets" (no pun intended) and maybe even ask her to come over and sit or lie awhile because you are a firm believer in that old adage "keep your friends close and your enemies closer," because the moment she appeared on your radar, she became red-level alpha threat number one!

D. Remember that it's totally okay to point out the obvious and compliment another woman's beauty, feeling confident that acknowledging her will in no way diminish your own beauty, and just wait a few minutes for the waters to again recede and the gulls to stop singing as you get up and take your glorious stride to and from the waters!

Answer: D. Good job, ladies! She is but a small blip on

the screen, and you should in no way do anything that will make her a larger part of what is you and your man's great day at the beach. He's there with you because he wants to be. If he were looking for her, he would have come alone! Trust that you are looking and feeling your best and that what you have is enough!

1. Ladies, you have been looking forward to your hair appointment all week. There's this new cut you can't wait to show off at the party you and your man have been looking forward to this weekend. When you arrive at the salon, unfortunately, you are made aware that your regular stylist is not there ... gulp. Nevertheless, you persevere. You are willing to take a chance on a new stylist. As the session ensues, you notice that she seems to be cutting off a lot more than you thought was necessary to achieve the desired effect. Not only that, but you agreed to let her add a splash of color to your hair as well. In the end, your new stylist calls over a second stylist to your chair, and you can see the pained look of horror in their eyes as they speak in brief hushed tones just to the side of you. Yes, ladies, the unthinkable has happened! Not only is it not the look you were going for, but it also is an absolute train wreck, in your opinion. Your hair is an interesting shade of orange and red you had previously only seen on orangutans on the Discovery channel. Your haircut is not so much "today's woman" but more like "eighteenth-century Spanish monk"! What's the first thing you say to your man when you see him?

A. How does my hair look? (Then wait for what will seem like an eternity of uncomfortable silence as your man stands frozen in his tracks desperately trying to find a word, a phrase, or a kind sentiment even, to end what is a highly combustible situation.)

B. I'm in here! (As you call him to come to your bedroom where you lie in your "sick bed" covered up in your

sheets—as my friends from the country would say "layin'
up sorry"—as you have actually felt physically ill and
nauseated since you returned from your adventure at
the salon today. You ask your man to please put on some
Norah Jones and slide you some Cherry Garcia ice cream
through the cracked door, as you will not be available to
him or the general public for the next few days, or until
your regular stylist gets back!)

C. Where are you going? (That's the second thing you say to
him because the first thing you say to him is "do you like
my hair," and he then makes an immediate U-turn and
abrupt exit as panic swells within him, and he mumbles to
you about forgetting something at work or in his car.)

D. Let me tell you what happened. (You begin to relay to
him the events of the day as they unfolded, and you
explain how you and your hair got to this point.)

Answer: D. Ladies, it is what it is—an unfortunate
happening. Don't compound the situation by pulling your man
into what is already a highly emotionally charged topic for you.
You could possibly end up with not only a bad hairstyle (if you
can call it that) but also an argument with your man. Just tell
him what happened and how disgusted you are with the results.
He will understand. Later on, while you shop for a new scarf
or cute hat to wear to that party, you may even be able to laugh
about it together.

What Not to Say

Ladies, in this chapter I'm going to give you a little something to take with you on your dating trail. Just keep these in your bag, and remember to *never* take them out unless you are intentionally looking for an argument or just trying to screw with our heads. Let's see if some of these sound familiar.

Where is this going?

If we knew, we'd tell you. If we knew and wanted you to know, too, we'd tell you. If it's not something we bring up, then the safe assumption here is that we really don't know.

Here's my advice: If you're really interested in finding out where he thinks this is going, then start that conversation by telling him where you think it's going and watch for his reaction … or lack thereof.

Are we lost?

Yes, dear, we are. And thank you for making me feel even more inadequate by clarifying that point. Can we just get some directions and move on?

Here's my advice: At this point, guys have gone into "survival go mode" Most rational thought has been left at the last mile marker. It's now up to you ladies to add some calm and reason to this situation. Suggest that you need to pull over at the nearest gas station so you can use the restroom, get a snack, or make up some other excuse. While there, casually ask your friendly neighborhood cashier just where in the heck you are. Beautiful in its simplicity.

So, your friend Stephen, the man-whore—you guys hang out a lot, huh?

Yes, dear, he's a close friend. And just because we hang out a lot does not mean we share some of the same whoring ways. I could just be his strong wingman, I could be there to help keep him out of some sketchy situations, or, alas, dear heart, I too could be a friend of many loose women. Whatever the situation is, it's not like I'm ever going to tell you the truth, no matter how many times or different ways you ask that same question.

Here's my advice: Men know that most women judge us by the company we keep—which is probably a smart thing to do. However, most men will become immediately defensive when asked about their past or current associations with any "undesirables." Defensive for us means there will be no answers for you. Ladies, you can simply state that you understand how some men go through a phase where they need to sow their wild oats, and ask him if he feels that he's past that stage. Now that you've somewhat normalized that behavior in his mind, he will be more willing to give you a calm, rational, and truthful answer.

You gonna wear that?

Yes, damn it! I thought it looked good, but evidently I'm wrong. Now, I have to wear it to wherever we are going, just to prove a point to you. What that point is, I'm not exactly sure, but it will be proven tonight nonetheless, as I proudly sport this too-small yellow, orange, and green muscle T-shirt with a screened picture of a peacock on the front and my old high school football number on the back (I was a "fighting cock," damn it!)!

Here's my advice: Some men, myself included, are highly particular about their wardrobes and their looks and have a great eye for fashion. Alas, most men do not. It's just not something men traditionally put a lot of thought into. So, you have to jumpstart most men's thought processes here. I suggest you start asking early about exactly where you will be going and what you will be doing this evening "just so you'll know what to wear" or "so you can try to dress to match him." This will cleverly open the door for you to do a preemptive strike and ask him what he's planning on wearing ... nice, right? That gets him to at least think about it and also gives you an opportunity to subtly shape and mold his attire for the evening as you tell him what you're wearing and tell him how much you like that [insert acceptable article of his clothing here] of his so much ... a deft touch, ladies!

What are you doing next Saturday morning?

Sleeping, if I'm at peace. But from the tone of your voice, it sounds like I will be busy moving something for somebody, shopping, antiquing, going on a spontaneous road trip, or attending some family/work function of yours that you don't want to be alone for. Whatever the case may be, sadly for me, I will not be at peace.

Here's my advice: Ladies, for men. Saturday mornings are like your most private dreams, your deepest secrets, or some or your makeup techniques—they are protected! For us, they are sacred! They represent a whole new realm of possibility (even though we're probably just gonna do the same thing we do most Saturdays, which usually involves the gym, a car, or a sports-related activity). Ever notice how sometimes your man just seems aggravated for no particular reason when you are spending time doing whatever on some Saturdays? Some of us are resentful because you're now cutting into our "protected time." Be really careful here of what you demand that he do with you or for you on Saturdays, and in the spirit of true bipartisanship, at least acknowledge that he may have other plans by saying "I know you probably have something to do, but I would really appreciate it if you had a little time to do [whatever "it" is here]. And, for Pete's sake (whoever Pete is), put a time limit on it!

I didn't realize you were that short.

Damn you; damn you to hell for that.

Here's my advice: First, don't say that. It's just downright hurtful. Second, you should have had an idea at the onset, if he did or did not meet your minimum height requirement, so why is that an issue now? Are you feeling dissatisfaction from another area of your relationship, and it's coming out as a sudden need to express disappointment about his height? If it's truly that critical of an issue for you, then I suggest you both look into some different shoe options (more heel for him/less heel for you) or some elongating colors for him (as in black). Or maybe you should just date someone who is taller! Seriously, you cannot ask us to change something that is impossible for us to change. If a guy is 5'5" today, he is pretty much gonna be 5'5" tomorrow. If his height is a source of embarrassment, disappointment, or frustration for you, then first, really examine why this is, and then, do both of you a favor and find someone who is more in line with your linear requirements.

Has your hair always looked like that?

Like what? What are you saying? Is it messed up? Is it thinning? Is it receding? Is it gray somewhere? Just what the hell are you saying? Again ... damn you!

Here's my advice: Remember, ladies: hair is not our forte. Not only are most of us clueless about your hair but also about our own. That's why most men are forever grateful to barbers! They're something akin to magicians. They come out, throw a big sheet over us, and presto change-o, we come out looking presentable! Here's a sad but true thought, ladies. Most men have been getting the same form of haircut since they were five years old! Seriously, again, it's not our forte. Ladies, if you want to change our look here, then simply suggest it. Better yet, show us a picture of a good-looking guy in a magazine with that hairstyle, tell us how much you think we look like him, and then march us to the nearest barber/stylist. You have no idea (because most of us won't admit it) how much we will eternally appreciate you for this! This is one area where our feelings won't get hurt (much) when you suggest a change. Ladies, in this arena, consider us to be dying of thirst. It's your task to lead us to a riverbed, so we might drink!

You're going out with the boys again?

Yes, damn it. That's where I was when I met you, and if this keeps up, it'll probably be where I am after we break up. Let me be. Can a man get a little break around here?

Here's my advice: If a man is still in that phase where he has to spend time out with boys, then there is precious little you will be able to do to change his thought process. It is what it is, and he is who he is. As a woman, just be your cute, playful, doting, lovable self, and gradually we will be drawn to you and want to spend more and more time with you. Careful now; don't get too frustrated if we don't come along as fast as you want. Remember, it is what it is. It has to do more with his thought process, not yours. If and when he decides to value time with you as much as, or more than, time with the boys, it will be a decision he comes to on his own. Remember "Saturday mornings"? If going out with the boys falls under his "protected time," then it will be a source of friction in the relationship, and you're definitely gonna have to pick your battles here.

Don't stop. Keep going. I'm almost there!

Sorry, babe, but I must stop now. My muscles (whichever

ones I may be using at this point) have grown tired and weary, and I must rest and be refueled. I did keep going ten minutes ago when you were "almost there." Now, I don't care where you're trying to go; I'm just going to sleep … after I fix myself a sandwich and watch a little sports center … lol … (that was for you, guys; I champion you still.)

Here's my advice: Ladies, there are few things that will bring a man greater joy in a relationship than being sound in the knowledge that he has totally, completely, and utterly satisfied you sexually. Here's the problem: he may not know how. I mean, he may know how to do it, but he just may not know exactly how to do it to you! Solution: tell him! It's just that simple. Be open and honest early about what you like and what you don't like and what really "gets you there" sexually. Don't be shy or embarrassed about what you want and what you like. The longer you go without talking about it, the harder (and then softer … sorry) it will become to bring it up. It's similar to the haircut situation. In the end, it's a bridge he will be glad you cared enough to cross, if it means that you're going to be more satisfied with him as your man.

Where were you last night?

Someplace you were not. Someplace, doing something I would prefer you did not know about. Someplace, doing something with someone or some ones that I would prefer you did not know about. The truth is, if I wanted you to know, I would have told you before I went. Since I did not, you can safely assume that, to know this secret, you'll have to pry it from my cold, dead hands.

Here's my advice: Touchy subject here. Do you want to know just because you're interested in how I spend my time when I'm not around you and want to make sure I'm doing things that are constructive and thoughtful, which will help me grow as a person? (Awwww … that's sweet of you.) Or, do you want to know because you're interested in just what kinds of destructive, thoughtless, point-lowering activities on the human scale I am engaging in when I'm not with you? Trust is the key here, ladies! Trust that you made a good choice in a man. Trust that you did your homework, asked the right questions, and are actively doing everything you believe you are willing and able to do as his woman to keep him satisfied. This is one of those times when you're going to have to do something that can be quite frightening. Trust him! Unfortunately, there are a lot of men who do things that you might find distasteful when you're not around. Fortunately, there are precious few men who can hide it well.

Surprise, honey; I have two tickets to the opera for tomorrow night!

Oh, blessed joy! You have no idea how many nights I lie awake feeling empty, yearning to hear loud singing in a foreign language, telling a story I'm totally uninterested in, to fill that void deep within me. Unfortunately, babe … I won't be able to attend. I have to go somewhere, anywhere, and do something, anything other than that. Ladies, we get it; it's classy, it's cultured, and it's conversational, but we're just not into it.

Here's my advice: Don't just spring it on us. Ask us if that is something we would be interested in before you pursue it. That way, we feel like we're along for the ride and not being held hostage! Also, aren't most events like this held on Saturdays? Damn! Protected time! Protected time! Most men are open to doing something classy and cultured, but we have to have some level of interest; otherwise, we're just going to be miserable the entire time. And if we're miserable—you guessed it—we're gonna try and make you just as miserable in some shape, form, or fashion. And it's not that we aren't interested in whatever it is. Oftentimes, it's that we may be uncomfortable in that setting and just don't want to say it. Communicate, compromise, and make it something you both would enjoy.

So, is Steve going to have strippers at his bachelor party?

Oh, my heavens, no! Perish the thought, dear. Scantily clad, overly friendly women who perform for money make us oh so uncomfortable. We'll probably just go out for a nice dinner, exchange honeymoon tips and ideas, and ponder the days when we so foolishly did engage in such things as being entertained by scantily clad, overly friendly women who do things for money—what were we ever thinking? Excuse me, honey, I have to return this text message from Candy and Porsche. They will be providing the… er … party favors for the tame, mild, all-male, non-stripperesque bachelor dinner we're having for our dear friend Steve.

Here's my advice: Pick your battles, ladies. I know most women are highly uncomfortable with the idea of their man being in an environment with scantily clad (okay, half-naked), openly flirtatious women with the added combustible element of alcohol. Again, here's where trust comes into play. Trust that your man will not do anything that you would disapprove of. Trust that he will not do anything disrespectful to you or your relationship. At the very least, trust that he is smart enough to not do anything that would put you at risk or otherwise in harm's way.

You think she's prettier than I am?

Yes. Yes, I do. And apparently so do you, or you wouldn't have asked the question. Most men and God Almighty think she's prettier than you. Otherwise, why would God have placed her here today in my direct line of sight while I'm here with you? You see, God likes to torment me in just this sort of way!

Here's my advice: Point out the obvious. Recognize her for her beauty, and simply move on. At this point, it's not so much about how pretty she is but more about how pretty you may think you are not.

It's okay, honey. I hear that happens to a lot of guys.

Nooooo! Not to me! Look, for whatever reason we couldn't deliver on the performance tonight, please don't compound the problem by patronizing us and attempting to excuse our lack of manhood. We'd rather you just got pissed and bid us a good night. Leave us alone to wallow in the shallow pond of our embarrassment. The more you talk about it, the harder (or maybe softer) it's gonna be next time. Please don't put that undue game pressure on us; it's enough to break a guy!

Here's my advice: Kid gloves, ladies, kid gloves! Nothing cuts to the root of a guy's manhood as his ... well ... man-root (sorry, I've read that word in numerous Harlequin romance novels but so rarely get a chance to use it. I have five sisters ... sorry). If it's just a onetime or rare occurrence, don't worry about it. If it gets to be routine, ask if there's anything you are or are not doing to help. Don't make it seem like it's all his problem (even though it may be). We need to know you are a part of our team here, ladies. Quite frankly, oftentimes impotence can have many causes (medical problems, medication side effects, fatigue, etc.). Rarely is it because he is unhappy in the relationship and is becoming resentful toward both you and himself for continuing it; rarely is it because he is no longer interested in pleasing you in any way and this inherent unwillingness to please you is now manifesting itself as his recurrent impotence.

My ex used to ...

Stop! Anything your ex used to say or do we are not concerned about (unless it was something like doing bodily harm to any guy he thought you were interested in). If he's your ex, then let him be that—exed! If what he used to do or say was so damn memorable, then maybe he should be here with you now instead of me. The "ex-chisel" is a tool that can chip away at a fresh relationship. Let sleeping dogs lie. If we're going to be together, then let's do that—be together.

Here's my advice: When you go on a trip, do you bring every piece of old luggage you've ever used on previous trips? No, you pack accordingly and use only what is needed and what's current. It would be virtually impossible to make it through a trip with that kind of old baggage. Same idea when you're venturing into a new relationship. Don't bring any baggage from your old relationships along for the ride. If we're doing something not to your liking, then let us know. But please don't compare us to your ex while doing it. If we're doing something that is to your liking, then let us know. Again, please don't compare us to your ex while doing it. If you're with us now, then we need your mind here, with us! Flip the coin here and imagine how uncomfortable and frustrated you would feel if we were constantly comparing you to our ex. What would you say to us? Now, stop and tell yourself the same.

Pop Quiz:
1. Here it is, ladies. Your new man has been out of town on business for the last week, and he is finally coming home tonight. You can't wait to see him, and he's been text-messaging you sweet nothings for the last three days. You plan a very relaxing and romantic dinner at home to make his return special. You and your girls have spent the day at the spa, and you are looking quite spectacular, if you do say so yourself. To top it off, you've picked up a little something special from Vickie's Secret in his favorite color! Tonight's gonna be a good night! He may be tired from his delayed flight, but after seeing you, he should become energized! The time is right, the mood is right, the moment is here, and the Victoria has told her secret! Just one small problem: there's a limp, flaccid, motionless appendage lying in the place where your man's throbbing, hard erection should be! How do you handle this, ladies?

A. Ask, "What's wrong? Why can't you get it up? Is it gonna take long? Do you want me to help?"
B. Say, "I'm sure your long week and delayed flight must

have contributed to your erectile dysfunction tonight. We can just try again in the morning once you've had some rest. Poor baby."

C. Say, "I knew it, you son of a bitch! You were probably screwing your little tramp down on the first floor in customer service all week and now can't do shit when you get back here to me! Maybe she's cute enough to get a rise out of you because I damn sure can't lately! Bastard!"

D. Say and do nothing initially. Remember the chapter your read in Dr. Major's book about what not to say in testy moments in a relationship? This qualifies as a testy moment.

Answer: D. Great, ladies! I congratulate you on handling this situation well. You remembered in the book that it said there are many problems that trigger impotence. First, take the pressure off of him by remaining calm. If and only if he offers an explanation or invites a discussion should you engage in problem solving at this point. This is one of those rare moments, ladies, where silence can truly be golden. Nicely done.

2. Ladies, you and your man are doing some shopping at this new outdoor mall one Saturday morning. You're having a great time, and you're particularly pleased that not only did he not have "something to do" this Saturday, but he also is enjoying the occasion and being quite patient with the whole shopping process. You have been having a conversation about how none of your former boyfriends were really that much into shopping. You also lament that you had to meet a lot of guys before finally finding him, but you're glad you kept looking. You then sneak in the fact that you did not have sex with most of the guys you've met in the past, "only a handful." Then you do it. You say it! You ask, "So, how many women have you slept with before me?" Your man immediately responds with a cleverly placed "huh?" You repeat the question. This time, he stumbles and

almost trips on the tile floor at the BeBe store (which seems awfully jagged all of a sudden … they really should fix that … a man could get hurt!). You stand firm, determined to wait for his answer. He makes an effort to answer. "I'm not sure. I've met a lot of girls, but I didn't sleep with most of them either." (Nice save!) However, you find that somewhat peculiar because you know of at least five women he has slept with in the past year who were in your formerly close circle of friends. What do you think, ladies? What do you think?

A. Awww. That's nice; he must have pretty much only slept with those few women I already know about. He's such a good boy!

B. Hmmm. I guess he must have just really started looking for someone pretty seriously this last year. I'm so glad he found me, because now he doesn't have to look anymore!

C. That lying son of a bitch! He couldn't even hide it! I remember hearing about him from my former best female friends, and they each spoke of at least three different women that they knew he had been with so that's three times five, which is at least fifteen, and that's just in this town. He's also lived in New York, Los Angeles, and Miami! Oh, my God! I'm dating a male whore! Why didn't they tell me?

D. Think nothing of his answer, and wonder to yourself why you even asked.

Answer: D. You remember from this book that men will often lie about the actual number of women they have had sex with, mostly because they just don't want to give you the wrong impression of them. You also remember that as long as you have enough information to be sure that he was safe in his practices, then the actual number, whether great like "the Mississippi" or small like a teacup, doesn't matter. He's with you now, and things are great, and that is all that matters to you.

First Comes Love

Okay, here's where the true love comes into play. Ah, hell, some of y'all were in love by the end of the first "meeting" chapter. But no matter; we press on. The best place to start is with a definition of the word. What is love? Merriam-Webster's dictionary defines it as this:

love:
1 **a** (1): strong affection for another arising out of kinship or personal ties <maternal *love* for a child> (2): attraction based on sexual desire: affection and tenderness felt by lovers (3): affection based on admiration, benevolence, or common interests <*love* for his old schoolmates> **b:** an assurance of love <give her my *love*>
2: warm attachment, enthusiasm, or devotion <*love* of the sea>
3 **a:** the object of attachment, devotion, or admiration <baseball was his first *love*> **b** (1): a beloved person: *darling*—often used as a term of endearment (2) *British*—used as an informal term of address
4 **a:** unselfish loyal and benevolent concern for the good of another: as (1): the fatherly concern of God for humankind (2): brotherly concern for others **b:** a person's adoration of God

5: a god or personification of love
6: an amorous episode: *love affair*
7: the sexual embrace: *copulation*[7]

Pretty good. I'm partial to #4, "the unselfish, loyal, and benevolent concern for the good of another." True, but love is more than just concern, isn't it? It's more than just those tender feelings of affection. Love, to me, is a collection of thoughts, feelings, and actions. If we liken a relationship to a play being acted out on a stage I think love would be those series of acts played out on that stage. We get to play the leading roles! I believe love is, first, the act of choosing someone and being chosen in return by that person. This act is followed by the act of caring enough to find out about what that person likes, wants, and needs in life. Then, finally, love is the act of giving that person what he or she likes, wants, and needs every day. Every day.

Shakespeare was so eloquent when he wrote "all the world's a stage/and all the men and women merely players/They have their exits and their entrances/And one man in his time plays many parts." Profound wisdom here! Of course, he wasn't specifically referring to our topic of discussion, but I believe the truth of his metaphor can be applied here as well. All the world's relationships evolve in "acts" and phases, and, also, sometimes it feels like we're on stage when in love. We all do our best to play our parts. The neat thing about this play is that we don't have to be master thespians to perform it well. We simply have to care about our costar. Love should be easy. Love should be simple. We all have a right to it. We all must do right by it. One of my favorite definitions of love comes from the movie *Don Juan DeMarco*. Johnny Depp plays a young man who believes he is the world's greatest lover, Don Juan. Marlon Brando plays his psychiatrist trying to cure him of his delusion. In the movie, Don Juan asks a series of questions: "What is sacred? Of what is the spirit made? What is worth living for? What is worth dying for?" The answer to each is the same—only love. Simply beautiful.

The lies we tell when we are in love are basically of two types. First, the lies of omission, or the things we will not tell you. Second, the lies we all tell ourselves. Both are powerful tools that can and often do cause long-term disruption and possible destruction of a family unit.

The Lies of Omission

"How was your day, baby?" "Fine." "How are you today, baby?" "Fine." "How are things at work, sweetie?" "Fine." "Babe, you seem a little aggravated. Is everything okay?" "Everything is fine." Ladies, ever been at that stage in a relationship where this was the answer to almost every question you asked? Frustrating, isn't it? Well, like I said, the lie isn't in what we're saying; it's more in what we're not saying. At this point, something clearly is wrong with the partner in this scenario. It could be work, could be family, could be financial, or it could be you. The problem is that you'll never know, because he refuses to give you an honest answer. Unacceptable! Even if he doesn't have an answer, he can still make the effort. More often than not, in relationships gone bad, it's the things left unspoken rather than the things that are said, that cause the most damage. When things are left unsaid, one thing this causes is doubt. What could it possibly be? Could it be something with me? The next thing it causes is resentment—resentment because your lover is refusing you his feelings and is closing the door to communication with his abrupt, one-word answers.

Also, there's supposed to be a basic trust here. Does this mean he doesn't trust you to handle what he has to say with care, concern, and love? There may be much to be discussed, but now may not be the right time, ladies. Give him a little space here, and say something like "I'm here to listen if you wanna talk about it." That will go over very well, because you are respecting his current decision to not share but are allowing him the opportunity to change his mind and open up in the future. Generally, in the next twenty-four hours, you'll probably hear more about whatever "it" was than you ever cared to know!

Sometimes, you have to take a small step backward to move two or three steps forward. The important thing here, ladies, is to let him know you recognize that something is wrong and that you also are aware that he does not wish to share that with you at this time. As guys, we understand that women know more about relationships and emotions than we do. We also know that you know when something is wrong or bothering us. We go on to believe that you expect us to share that with you. It's that expectation that puts the pressure on us (even if you haven't pressured us at all). It's that pressure that makes us want to retreat. It's that pressure that makes us not want to even think about whatever it is. By letting us know you understand and aren't trying to make us talk about it, you have relieved the pressure! Once the pressure is off, we naturally feel more at ease discussing openly whatever the issue may be!

The Lies We Tell Ourselves

One of the first lies we tell ourselves at this stage, when in love, is done so in grand fashion, in front of man and God. It's the one we tell in a church, on a beach, or on a cliff (which is quite telling by the way ... already close to the edge). It's when we say "I do" when we clearly don't.

Here's a hypothetical situation for you to ponder. There's this guy. Nice guy, very attractive, tall, handsome, and college educated to boot. Perhaps you know someone like him? At any rate, he was recently married. For him, his newlywed year was pure bliss. Spontaneous trips out of town. Regular gatherings and get-togethers out and about with friends. More phenomenal, wild, crazy, multi-partner sex than he ever dreamed of or imagined was possible!

Unfortunately for his wife, sweet innocent dear that she is, none of these things he was doing involved her. He said "I do" when clearly he shouldn't have. Why? I thought you might ask that. I think part of it is fairly simple. This man is still a wee bit immature and just a bit selfish ... okay ... maybe a lot selfish. He needs to have a deeper understanding of himself. This situation illustrates the reality of the person we are, confronting the promise of the person we want to become. This man is a good man. Loves his mom, came from a good family, has a steady and good-paying job, college educated, very attractive, and the word on the street from some of his ex-girlfriends ... er ... current girlfriends (ummmm, not really sure what to call them; technically, can you have a girlfriend if you're already married?) is that he's fairly decent in the bedroom. So yes, on paper, he's a great guy who has always wanted to grow up and have a loving, caring, long-lasting relationship with the one woman he loves. That's who he has always wanted to be—that guy. However, the reality of who he is today is just a bit different. The reality is this: Today, his actions are those of a man who is not interested in a mature, monogamous relationship. Today, he is man who cheats on his wife. He considers himself to be this and is unsure if he can or if he is even willing to change his behavior at this time.

Now, the reality of who he is today doesn't preclude him from ever becoming that loving, doting husband he has always wanted to be. He can still be that guy. He just has some growing up to do. How nice it would have been for his wife and their future children if he had been honest with himself and waited until he had put that "loving, doting husband wrench" in his toolbox and had put that "man-whore hammer" on the shelf. But this situation is not all his fault, ladies. I have to ask you, what is it about you that makes you not want to see or admit to yourself who this guy is? Did you honestly not know? Did you have no clue of what he was capable of? And if so, why? Is this guy really that smooth and charming that he's just pulling the wool over your eyes, and you're totally oblivious to his transgressions? Or were you so convinced that he was "the one" that you were willing to forgive or look the other way, in hope that once he made the commitment to you, he would change? Remember, when it comes to a man's behavior in a relationship, there are two people playing parts.

Again, we have to take an honest inventory of where we are in life and see how that matches up with where we think we might want to go. In short, we all need to be as sure as sure can be before we drag someone into the consequences of our uncertainty. When I was a child, there was a cartoon show that used to come on Saturday mornings called *Schoolhouse Rock*, with neat little jingles and colorful cartoon characters to help teach children lessons that could be difficult for their minds to grasp. I remember one episode in particular, called "I'm just a bill." It was a caricature of a bill that was on the long, hard road of trying to become a law. With childlike simplicity, this bill talks about the long, hard journey he has to undertake to become a more mature, more adult law. Yes! He understood! He understood that, in order for him to become who he wanted to be, he had to grow. He had to change. He was willing to put in the work and be patient in the interim. Sage wisdom from the pages of this kiddie "book" of knowledge.

The bill longs to become more; he wants to become a law. However, he is under no delusions whatsoever about exactly where and who he is right now, today; he's just a bill. He understands that to become more, he has to go through a process of growth. As men we all long to be more, to be something greater that what we are—a noble goal. However, we must not get this confused with who we are today, right now, at this moment in time. The hypothetical character from the example above also longs to be more; he wants to become a law. He hopes and prays that he will, but today he is still just ... not.

Also, we can't allow ourselves to become blinded by the brilliant light of the other person. Some people say, "I got married because I knew she was the one, and I didn't want her to get away." Well, that's all well and good, she very well may be the right one, but you should first ask "is this the right time?" Timing is a critical element to the whole commitment process. Everything here has to flow smoothly, like fine wine; if opened at the wrong time, you just get a bunch of sour grapes. Ladies, he may be the one. He may be "that guy." The butterflies you feel when you think of him may be unlike any you've ever felt before. You may see in him, the potential to become everything you've ever wanted and needed in a man. But it is going to take time and energy in order for that potential to manifest. Unfortunately, love doesn't run on *potential* energy. It only runs on *real* energy—real time and real energy that you both are putting into the relationship today!

I have a colleague who is a single, African American, male physician, never married, and with no children, who is exceptional with money. He is often asked, "Why aren't you married?" His answer is simple and brazenly true: "I just don't see what that would add to my life right now." Amazing! He's happy with who he is and where he is in life right now today, and he makes decisions based around those facts ... what a concept! This just belies the point that we have to be comfortable with who we are and where we are before we bring someone else into that dynamic. It's only right. It's only fair—to you and to them.

Remember to Ask about the Little Things

As we get deeper into a loving relationship, the things we need to know evolve. By now, we've figured out each other's favorite dish, favorite movie, favorite thing to do to relax, and favorite things to do whatever, whenever, however. What we need to know and what you need to know, ladies, now becomes quite specific: small questions that in most bad marriages go unasked. I call them "Christmas Tree questions." I call them this because there is a classic case that is used to teach psychiatry residents about the subtle aspects of relationships. The case goes like this: There is a young couple in marital therapy, and they divulge that their first and most traumatic argument ever was over what color lights to place on their Christmas tree. She had grown up with and was a fan of the clear lights, but her husband was a red-light, green-light kind of a guy. They both said "this is the way we've been doing it since I was a kid, and this is just the way we're gonna keep doing it!."

Argumentative statements and general marital discord ensued at that point. There was no emotional resolution that night. The practical resolution that they came up with was to use both sets of lights, both indoors and outdoors. The outcome here, while it should be praised for its compromise and emotionally settling effects, should be jeered for probably resulting in the most hideously decorated tree and home on the block that season. But at least they tried. And they stayed together—because they took this situation and extrapolated it to other areas of their lives. They began to ask, "Gee, I wonder what else we didn't ask each other before we got married?" They spent the bulk of their therapy finding out those types of things.

It was amazing to see, as week after week, they would ask more questions and find out more about each other. An interesting thing happened: they fell more in love with each other. Whoa! What a concept they had stumbled upon. Ask specific questions about your partner, and listen intently to the answer (as if it will affect your life … because it actually will). Then, have a dialogue about it. Are we going to have our kids accept our religion, or are we going to let them seek and find their own faiths in their own way? Are we going to send our kids to private or public school? Turkey or ham for Christmas dinner (trust me, it's a big deal!)? Holidays with your family or mine? Showers in the morning or at night before we go to bed? Sex with the lights on or off (that's actually a pretty big question too; there are so many issues of self-confidence and body image realities and distortions wrapped up in that one seemingly simple question that it would take another book to really explain it)? these are seemingly benign questions until you realize your partner thinks differently. These are just examples of simple questions that, if you let them catch you unaware, can be quite difficult to navigate with tact and without hurting your partner's feelings. One of the themes of this book is for you not to ignore the obvious. Also, please do not overlook or take for granted the simple.

Pop Quiz

1. Ladies, lately you've noticed that your husband has been making some changes. He's started working out more, has taken an interest in new things (things he previously had little to no interest in), has changed his views on a few subjects, has updated his wardrobe, and has even switched from boxers to boxer briefs. He's also been having to work longer hours at work. You don't think any of this is suspicious, because you know he's up for a big promotion at work, and part of that new position will include projecting a strong image. You're proud of him for making the effort. At the next company function, the spouses are invited for a "meet and greet" of the higher-ups. You also are surprised to meet your husband's new assistant, Nicky—surprised because you didn't even know he had a new assistant, although she sure seems to know a lot about you. She knows where you're from, how you met your husband, where you went to school, and even the names and ages of your children. By the way, did I mention that Nicky is devastatingly cute, nauseatingly bubbly, young, firm, and new? Well, she is. What do you think, ladies? What do you think?

A. No big deal. The company is notorious for hiring fly-by-night assistants who meet those criteria, as you feel they are overly image conscious. Once the promotion is decided, she'll be gone like yesterday's news.

B. You're actually pleased, because clearly Nicky's attention to detail and the zest she brings to the job will be just the trick your husband needs to ensure he gets that well-deserved promotion. He might even surprise you with that cute little number from the Mercedes lot once he gets promoted. Joy!

C. You become concerned but not worried. You take the initiative to find out a little more about Ms. Nicky and just how much time she and he spend together at work and just how much of your husband's new attitude is coming from her.

D. You're petrified! You've often lamented your husband's roving eye and are dismayed because little Ms. Nicky seems like she's just his type! It sickens you to see just how familiar they seem to be around each other, and you're starting to think there may be something to the whispers you've been hearing from the other company wives. Your intuition is starting to give you that sinking feeling.

Answer: D. Be afraid, ladies. Be very afraid! Nicky is powerful, and your husband is weak. Her pimp hand is strong, and your husband is but a disadvantaged "working girl" on the corner. She is a king to his rook. She is a Ferrari to his smart car. She is Goliath! She is Sampson! Ladies, she is Rambo—your worst nightmare, and she's coming to get you!

You must pay close attention to what's going on here. Obviously, trust your husband to not do anything to jeopardize your relationship. Obviously, trust that Nicky will do everything in her power to get what you have. Do not, I repeat, do not belittle little Ms. Nicky, because your jealousy and envy of her only endear her to him more. What you can do is begin to innocuously point out the changes your husband has been making to himself, as he honestly may not be aware of the meaning behind them. Your biggest weapon in this battle royale will be trust! The trust you have in your husband's judgment. The trust you have in yourself as a loving and devoted wife. The trust you have in the firmness of your relationship. Remember, try as we might, ultimately we cannot control other people. We can only control ourselves and our own thoughts and actions. Trust that what you have is good and sacred, and gently remind your husband of the same because honestly ... sometimes we forget.

2. You're coming up on your one-year anniversary! Congratulations! The year wasn't easy, but you got through it. On the one hand, certain things couldn't be better. You're married to a handsome, smart, and very successful doctor. Your mini-mansion home is simply fabulous! You just love the way the seats in your new Mercedes can not only heat but also cool your derriere at the mere push of a button. You've been able to quit your job and become a stay-at-home wife. All the other ladies turn green with envy when you show up for your Pilates classes always looking so young, fresh, and new! But ... there's always a "but," on the other hand, your family is still not convinced that your husband was the marrying type. Your best girlfriends are politely but constantly telling you to keep your eyes on him and be careful. The ladies at the front desk in his office seem to give you the most peculiar looks whenever you walk in—not so much a look of jealousy or of simple friendliness, but more like a look of pity. Curious. Well, you pay it no mind. It's no secret that your new husband used to be a notorious womanizer. A young Hefner in training, if you will. He told you all about his past relationships, about when he was a man of a "lesser committed mind" and how he was ready to make a change once he met you. Having said that, you're home one Wednesday morning straightening up the pillows on the sofa in the day room a bit when you notice a brightly colored piece of material peeking out from under one of the cushions. Your nimble fingers give it a tug, and it turns out to be a cute little pair of thong panties. You chuckle to yourself as you think you must have forgotten you placed them there during

one of you and your new husband's more heated moments of passion. That chuckle quickly turns into a gasp as you realize that you recognize neither the color nor the design of this particular pair of panties (you never wear T-backs). And—oh my God—they're a size extra small, and you, dear wife, are a medium! What do you, ladies? What do you think?

A. Pay it no mind, as you remember your husband saying that he suspected your housekeeper, Issabella, may be having male company over when no is home. The two of you are going to have to sit her down and have a stern talk with her!

B. Pay it no mind, as you remember that your new tart of a sister-in-law recently house-sat for you while you and your husband were on vacation in Rio, and you're oh so sure that she must have been up to her antics again. The two of you are going to have to sit her down and have a stern talk with her!

C. Begin to wonder how you got to this point. You discard the evidence (I know, I know, some of you ladies are saying "no, girl! Don't throw them away! It's evidence!"). At any rate, you discard the evidence and vow that, from this day forward, you will pay more attention to your husband's habits and not turn a blind eye to what your family and friends have thought about him. You won't openly accuse him of wrongdoing at this point, but you're about to play prison warden to his "inmate number 000000-000." Straight lockdown! How did things ever get here?

D. Begin to wonder how you got to this point. You don't remember driving to the hospital, yet here you are in a hospital bed with your divorce attorney at one side with a moist towel for your forehead, and your mother and best girlfriend at your other side, feeding you apple juice and ice chips. You're so parched! You listen in shock as they recant the story to you of how you must have fallen and hit your head immediately after you called them and told them about what you had found. Oh, yes, the impromptu business trips, the long hours working late, the check card receipts for dinners for two that you never attended, your husband's extensive and prized *Girls Gone Wild* DVD collection … it's all coming back to you now! How did things ever get here?

Answer: C. Just a harsh reminder that "all that glitters ain't gold"! In looking back, her husband clearly lied to himself about being ready to be in a mature and monogamous relationship. In looking back, she clearly lied to herself about who the man she had been dating and had married actually was. In looking forward, they both are going to need to take an honest inventory of where each of them are in life and decide if they want to try to move forward with each other. There's no shame in making mistakes in the past. Just make sure you don't continue to make those same mistakes in judgment as you move forward in life.

3. You and your husband had an argument last night. You felt bad about it all day today and decided to come home from work early to get started on a "makeup dinner" and ready yourself for what you hope will be a night of "makeup sex." You come home, only to find that your husband has the same idea: make-up sex. Unfortunately for you, he's in your bed, having it with your best girlfriend! What do you do, ladies? What do you do?

A. You go to the closet, and brandish your firearm, because you remember the last conversation you had with your friend, John, who's a lawyer. He said that, in the event that something like this ever happened, you may, in fact, be able to kill both of them at the same time and get away with it. You remember something vaguely about a "crime of passion" and wonder if you will get a makeup person before you go on CNN to tell your story.

B. Almost immediately, you get over your shock and dismay and tell your husband that if this is what he really wants, then you're willing to allow it. Then ask if you may join in the festivities (I am amazed at how many times this is actually the outcome!).

C. Leave the room, skip to the kitchen, finish preparing your meal, and eat, satisfied and giddy in the knowledge that you've just become newly single and the sole owner of your home, and that you will probably receive some sort of monthly stipend from what used to be your better half.

D. Take that frying pan in your hand, dump the chicken breast out, replace it with some part of your husband's head and your girlfriend's (or former girlfriend's) ass, and start to waling! After the ass whupping is complete, go down to the kitchen and calmly wait for them to scurry down and offer some sort of explanation. Then decide what, in fact, needs to happen in this marriage.

E. All of the above.

F. None of the above.

Answer: E. Or at least some combination of all of the above. I think the waves of emotion and thoughts here would be overwhelming to say the least, and I can't really offer the right way to handle this situation. It's going to be different for everyone. I will say that I do not condone violence and murder as feasible solutions to any problems (not that it wouldn't make you feel better, mind you). Here is where you really take a hard look at your life and the people in it, and make some hard choices about whether they are truly helping you or hurting you at this point. Some couples can recover from such indiscretions. Some crumble. There are so many variables that are in play that there really is no one right or wrong answer … once you get past the not-killing-them part …

4. Ladies, your sex life, while generally satisfying, has fallen victim to the imagination-zapping monotony of married life. You and your husband have used things in the past to spice it up a bit, such as toys, role-playing, change of locations, and a touch of exhibitionism mixed with a splash of voyeurism, all in the effort of maintaining a healthy and fulfilling sex life. You both have always been able to communicate openly and honestly in order to have your needs met in this arena. One night, he suggests what some might view as a radical idea. He asks if he may introduce a new toy to the routine—a dildo ... well, a strap-on to be exact—for you to use on him. You are initially confused as to where exactly you would use it on him because he doesn't have a vagina, and surely oral sex with a strap-on can't be all that gratifying, so just where ... oh ... there. Yes, ma'am. His backdoor. The impenetrable fortress, as it were. You grapple with the idea in your mind and reluctantly agree to proceed. Initially, wife, you are both amazed and dismayed. Amazed at the ease with which the strap-on repeatedly and completely penetrates your husbands anus, requiring surprisingly little thrust on your part (almost like this wasn't his first time). You are also dismayed at the newfound zest and verve with which your husband is actively participating in this session. Why, it seems that he grows more excited with each pump. Things reach a fevered pitch, and at one point, your husband slams his ass into you (and the strap-on) with such force that it actually knocks you off the bed and onto the floor. Oh, my. You use this floor time to do two things: one, to catch your breath because you didn't realize it was this much hard work from the other side, and two, to gather your thoughts and consider the true meaning of this evening's events. What do you think ladies? How do you feel?

A. No big deal, just one of those wifely duties that must be performed in the name of keeping your man happy.

B. Growing concern, as you realize you were really

turned on by the power you felt in holding dominion over your husband's ass and delivering blow after blow to what must be his most vulnerable area. Does this mean I wanna be a man, or do I have that penis envy thing I've read about?

C. Rising concern, as you had a sneaky suspicion that your husband may, in fact, have used such a tool before, as evidenced by his referring to it as "his bad boy Bobby" and by how amazingly adept he was at getting himself into positions and angles that would allow you to have maximum penetration. You may have a few more questions for him when this is over.

D. All-out panic; your fears have been confirmed. It's all coming flooding back to you now: long hours at the gym, always adhering to his strict dietary habits, weekly appointment to his hair stylist, his wearing the most fly boots ever worn by a man, his calling his style "metro" before anyone knew what metro meant, and, lastly, he still TiVos *Will and Grace*.

Answer: D! Ladies, do you ever wonder about those ladies who marry guys who "used to be gay but aren't gay anymore"? Well, you can officially stop wondering! What it was like for them is what it currently is like for you! Yes, woman. Your man … I won't say is gay or bisexual … I'll just say he fervently enjoys those activities typically reserved for only the gay or bisexual male. What this means, ladies, is it's up to you to figure it out. I will say that they often make comparisons to a man's anus and butterfly wings. They say butterfly wings, once touched, may never again be able to fly from the ground. They say a man's anus, once slammed by his wife with a strap-on, may never again be able to climb the road back to hetero-station or metro-center. Instead, he must walk the "down-low" roads encountering back doors at every turn and making only one stop in town—the closet! Where I'm sure, ladies, you wish he had stayed …

HAPPILY EVER AFTER ...

They say you never really know a person until you've lived with him or her. Some of you are saying right now "ain't that the truth!." I believe this to be true as well. When you live with someone, you get to see on a daily basis the real truth of who that person is. You get to know all the personality quirks, all the habits—some good and some bad. The true essence of who a person really is becomes a lot harder to hide at home. Note that I said *harder* to hide, but not impossible. It amazes me sometimes how married people who've been together for years sometimes still come to me with startling revelations about their mates. Is it that they couldn't see it? Or is it more that they didn't want to see and believe it? In truth, it's probably a bit of both.

I've been saying this throughout this whole book: sometimes, the obvious things are obvious. Case in point. A friend comes to see me, frantic. "Oh, my God, I don't know what I'm going to do. I think my husband is going to leave me." I try to be calming here. "Okay, let's sit down and talk about it. What happened that makes you think your husband is going to leave you?" She answers, "Because last night, he said 'I'm going to leave you!'" Obvious things are obvious. There is also such a thing as the square peg/round hole phenomenon. Simply put, everything isn't for everybody.

Here's a hypothetical situation for you to ponder. Imagine a man who, on his first wedding anniversary, was so overjoyed with marital bliss that he went out, got drunk, and had an affair in which the other woman (of a different race) became pregnant. He and his wife persevered. And on their second wedding anniversary, he was again so overcome with unbridled matrimonial nirvana that he went out, got drunk, and got thrown in jail (the charges were ... umm ... not pertinent to the story). Ladies, clearly here is a man who does not want to be married! Someone took a square peg and jammed it into a round hole, and it has been an awful fit ever since. He is acting out in the worst way. For whatever reason, he cannot express to his wife in words that he does not desire to be married, so he expresses these sentiments in actions ... hence, acting out.

Let me pause here and say that marriage is a beautiful thing! The sharing, the caring, the family roots you put down, and the family that grows from those roots—simply amazing. I tell patients and also friends that marriage is about remembering. You have to remember to respect each other. Remember that you care about each other being happy. Remember that you enjoy spending time together. Remember that you are interested in knowing what the other person thinks about things. Remember that this is the person whom you wanted to experience life with. Remember that you love each other. Isn't that why you got married? Well, it should have been. Not because of money issues, not because somebody got pregnant, and not because the other person was just so fine that you couldn't let him or her get away. All these things matter as well, but they are not lasting truths. That is to say, just because those things are true today does not mean they will be true tomorrow. The reasons for marriage should be quite simple and quite basic. You just have to remember to remember those things I mentioned above.

My parents have been married for fifty years now, and Lord

knows, it has not been easy. Ups, downs, trials, tribulations, working hard jobs with no retirement benefits at the end, raising seven children, and having nine grandchildren, all the while being an African American family in the deep South. It has not been easy, to say the least. But through it all, I don't think they would have chosen to go through it with anyone else but each other. They met when my mom was six years old, and my dad was eight. He likes to say he knew then but just kept his eye on her until she was older. How sweet is that? I have certain criteria for success. In my mind, my parents are two of the most successful people I know. They are successful for making the sacrifices they had to make and doing the things necessary to ensure that their children had everything they needed to go out into this world and be successful. They are successful for being able to enjoy an unlimited amount of love and respect from their family, as we are all so grateful for everything they have done.

However, this isn't the norm anymore, is it? These are the top five main reasons that people get divorced:

- Communication problems
- Financial issues
- Forms of abuse
- Sexual problems
- Marital infidelity[8]

Communication is a key issue. Sixty-eight percent of couples seeking counseling cite poor communication as their most common complaint.[9] There's a lot that can and often does go wrong in marriages. The lies we tell here are mostly lies to ourselves: "I guess I'm happy." "Things could be better, but they are all right." "I'm staying for the kids." "I can't afford to leave right now." "She's good for me." "We don't get along, but we balance each other out." "Well, I'm married, but I can have friends." And one of my all-time favorites: "I love her, but I'm not *in* love with her."

Well, these lies are all just excuses, aren't they? Excuses to continue to do the same thing you've been doing day in and day out that have not allowed you to be happy. It's human nature to look for reasons to justify our behavior in an attempt to help us better deal with the realities of our lives. Killers justify killing by saying "that person deserved to die." Thieves justify thieving by saying "they had enough and could afford to lose some of it." Cheaters justify cheating on their partners by saying "I'm not satisfied, and I deserve to be happy too." Oh yeah, and cheaters also say that the other person is "probably fooling around, too, but I just don't know about it." The rationales can be endless.

The truth is, that we are all adults, and as such, we make adult decisions and have to be able to live with the consequences. If we can't, that's when we begin to lie to ourselves in order to justify the things we do. Instead of making excuses to justify the things you do, why not try to take a moment and consider the reason for the unhappiness, and then work forward on a solution together from there? The key word here being *together*!

Financial issues seem to have taken the lead in a lot of people's lives these days. They can often be one more source of tension in a marriage. The tension can result from disappointment when someone thinks that his or her partner doesn't make enough money. Tension can also arise from frustration when, at the end of every month, you both realize that there isn't enough money to get all the bills paid and still have something left over. The tension can come from the fear that you honestly may not be able to afford your home, your car, or something else, as things become more and more expensive, and your pay stays the same. Some people say "money just isn't that important to us," or "we can live on love." Well, maybe *you* can, but the bank that holds your mortgage or the title to your car absolutely cannot!

Couples have to be willing to have honest discussions about lifestyle and the importance of material things, and they must attempt to adjust their habits accordingly. You basically have two options. Make more or spend less. Spending less? It is what it is. Be mindful of your budget, and plan ahead for unforeseen expenses. Make more? A few options here include furthering your education to attain a higher-paying job, starting your own business, working smarter at your current job to climb up the company ladder, or leaving the person you're with and trying to be with someone who makes more money. Financial issues present a harsh but true reality. Even though the last option mentioned above is one that I see exercised often, it is not one I can openly condone. Here, you have to be willing to really take a look at just how important to you those material status symbols are and what you may be willing to sacrifice to get them or keep them. An instructor of mine used to say "when people marry for money, they end up earning it every day."

The issues we bring into a relationship are often overlooked initially but usually end up rearing their heads at some point down the road. Issues of abuse fall into this category. Statistics report that at least one out of every four women in this country will suffer some type of abuse in her lifetime.[6] This can be verbal, mental, physical, or sexual abuse. These are the statistics for reported abuse, but I submit to you that the number may, in fact, be much higher, as the inherent shame and guilt often associated with abuse often keeps women from reporting it. And, unfortunately, there is typically a vicious cycle or pattern to abuse that can be dealt from one generation to the next.

Abuse can be one of the most difficult things in a person's life to ever deal with. But it can be dealt with! Does it take an unbelievable amount of courage and strength? Yes! Does it take much understanding and patience from those close to you? Yes! You have to believe that you can move forward! You have to know that, just because something awful was done to you, that's not all of who you are! My most sincere advice here is to not deal with it on your own. I advise that you get the proper professional help, probably starting with a good therapist. Oftentimes, these issues can affect you in ways you don't even realize, but once these things are pointed out to you, there is a much greater chance of overcoming them. And, in issues of abuse, sometimes that chance is all a person needs to do better.

Sexual frustrations can also be a huge problem in committed relationships. Someone's unhappy. But why? Is someone's technique not up to par? Is someone not getting … it … the way they like? Is someone, because of illness or medication, physically unable to perform? Is someone just unwilling to even go there, for whatever reason? It's interesting how a lot of men pride themselves on being able to separate sex from love while they're single but absolutely cannot do so once they get married. Issues with your partner outside of the bedroom will often follow you into the bedroom! The many reasons for couples being unhappy with each other sexually can warrant individual attention (speaking of warrants … maybe you should have him dress up like a cop and serve you with a warrant and then use some toy handcuffs once you resist arrest and … sorry … I digress). Whatever the source of the sexual frustration, one thing is for sure. It will absolutely not get better until the two of you are willing to sit down and have a conversation about it. If one person is thinking about a problem, then chances are pretty high that it's on his or her mate's mind as well. You must be willing to talk about the elephant that's in the room and sitting on your bed, as it were.

Here's a hypothetical situation for you to ponder. Let's say we have a young, attractive man in a very well-paid, very highly respected profession that encourages a lot of collegiality and requires a fair amount of social commitments. He becomes friendly with a colleague, starts dating her, and falls madly in love with her. They have common interests and common bonds and are seeing each other regularly with a mutual attraction. It was bound to happen. Everyone saw it coming—everyone except his wife and her husband!

It amazes me how infidelity can happen so routinely. The reason for the affair as stated, you might ask? "I'm not happy!" He wasn't happy at home and sought that happiness elsewhere.

A logical solution to this type of problem, you might say. The problem is in the timing: when does this solution come into play? Feel free to seek happiness elsewhere, but you have to be adult enough to first have tried to fix what was wrong at home. Did you give your spouse or partner a chance to do better? That means that you calmly sat and had a discussion about your feelings and what you felt was lacking in the relationship and what could be done to improve it. At this time, you also gave your spouse a chance to calmly tell you some of the things he or she felt were lacking, which you should work on as well. Then you also gave each other ample time to work on these things. This is good time to seek couples therapy, by the way. Then, lastly, if no progress was made by your spouse or you, then you found a way to conclude things in an adult and civil manner. I believe you should do all these things before you pull another person and both families into your search for happiness. It's only fair. Adult decisions. Adult consequences.

This, of course, is a hypothetical situation, but have you ever noticed in real-life situations resembling this one, that sometimes the outside relationship can grow to become the one of your most primary concern? Amazing how that happens, and the spouse is often left feeling like the outsider in the dynamic. The man is this scenario is no different from most, if not all, people who are in unhappy relationships. His brain is working on a way to make it better. His brain is seeking ways to find relief from suffering. The brain is constantly working on solutions to what people perceive as their problems—the key words being *your problems*. That is to say that *your* brain is first working to save *you* and *you* alone ... as it should ... I mean, it is your brain for God's sakes ... it owes you that much.

At any rate, you must be careful and be able to take an objective look at the possible solutions your brain will present to you. It's going to be your job to pepper these solutions with logic, rationalism, and ease of implementation. Also, don't be selfish. You are not the only one in the unhappy relationship.

My guess is that there is someone else on the other side of this situation who is quite miserable as well. The happiness of other people is also at stake. Other feelings can be hurt. And the decisions you make now will have a lifetime of consequences not just for you but for everyone involved. Adult decisions. Adult consequences.

Back to our scenario. How did it turn out? Well, he realized that he had some growing to do, so he took a real look at what was important to him and where he wanted his life to be, not just today but also tomorrow. He remembered! He remembered what it was about his wife that he admired, cared for, valued, and had fallen in love with. He remembered how much he adored their children and would do anything for them. He realized that he had a choice. He chose his wife, and his life has been nothing short of amazing from that day until now. Adult decisions. Adult consequences.

When It's Time to Let Go

One of my favorite songs is by an old-school R & B group L.T.D., with Jeffrey Osborne as the lead singer, called "Holdin' On." It speaks about the things we tell ourselves when we are in an unhappy relationship, to justify why we haven't done anything to change our situation. It also speaks about the emotional effects of being unhappy. Finally, this song speaks the simple truth that holding on can be extremely hard to do when the love has gone. I'm a huge fan of old-school logic because it's straightforward and to-the-point! Everyone who has been or is currently in a struggling relationship has probably felt and dealt with these kinds of emotions at some point. Holding on to a relationship when there is no love left can be excruciating. If done long enough, it robs you of who you are. It can rob you of your joy. It makes it hard to look forward to anything, because it will all involve that other person. The thoughts of that relationship or lack thereof can consume you.

At this point in a relationship is when I get to meet a lot

of my patients, as they seek both psychiatric and psychological help. At some point, you're going to have to deal with the reality and possibly the finality of the situation. You should remember to be true and fair to yourself at this point. Lie to yourself here, and you open the door to a lifetime of unhappiness, not just for you but for everyone involved. Be true to yourself here, even though it may be tough for the time being and may even cause you to struggle a little or even a lot. But in the end, in the long run, you will have made a choice that makes your life better and happier, and that is what gives you peace of mind. Some people say life is short, so have fun now and live it up. No, it's not. Life can be quite long, and it can feel downright eternal if you're having to live through some poor choices. One of the smartest quotes I ever read was from the book *Chicken Soup for the Soul*. It said that "people come into your life for a reason, a season, or a lifetime." That is so true! It goes on to explain how a situation can become so difficult when we try to hold on to a person past their time. Sometimes the best thing we can do is let go.

If the end is imminent, then bitterness can often be the pervading feeling in the house. Experts in this field call this the "pass the salt" stage. Let me set the scene: You and your husband are eating a quiet dinner (emphasis on quiet) at home. No eye contact is being made. The only chatter being made is the click-clack of your forks and knives hitting the plates. You're thinking about your stuff; he's thinking about his stuff. You ask him to "please pass the salt." He says, "Fuck you! You ruined my life, you evil bitch!" This is not quite the response you were expecting at this particular time but neither was it a total surprise. To put it mildly, he's taken issue with the way his life has turned out and the role he believes you have played in that outcome. To put it bluntly, he hates you! There is a lot that has to go unsaid to get to this point.

So, if you feel like a mess has been made, how do you clean it up? If the end is near, what now? How do we pick up the pieces and move on? The truth is, it depends on the situation. Some people have to make this decision based on safety—both their own and that of their children. Leaving here has to be done quickly, permanently, and with legal assistance. Sadly, more than one out of every four women in the United States have been or currently are in an abusive relationship.[6] Sometimes the leaving is more practical. Property has to be divided, careers have to be juggled for a time, and decisions have to be made in order to keep the children's lives from being totally disrupted. The luxury here, if there is one, is the time you have to really think about and make adult plans to help deal with the pending adult consequences. I'm always sad to see the disappointment in someone's eyes when he or she realizes that the person they thought was their true love turns out to be something … less. My psychotherapy instructor would say: "The problem with relationships is that, by the time we figure out we don't want to be with this person, it's already gonna hurt to pull away."

In the End, Love Wins

At this point, my hope is that I've provided you with enough information and examples to recognize a lie when you hear one. What is a lie? Simply put, it's something that isn't true. What does it take to construct a lie? Two things. First, a person willing to say something that is untrue. Second, a person willing to believe it. Remove either one of these from the equation, and the lie simply cannot exist! Since you know you cannot control another person, you must seek to control yourself. Prepare yourself to be that woman who can recognize a lie when she hears it and can choose not to believe it. Remove yourself from that liar's equation! I hope I've given you some tools to do just that.

Isn't it interesting that, no matter how difficult the breakup or ending of a relationship is, we almost always live to love again? It's like the famous line from *Jurassic Park*: "Life finds a way." With relationships, it's the same thing … love finds a way! And since chances are that love will find its way back into your heart, why don't you try to find a way to make it a more truthful journey? Remember, in the beginning, when I talked about the ingredients for a healthy relationship? Respect each other every day. Trust each other every day. Be honest with each other every day. Support each other every day. Try to be fair with each other every day. Communicate effectively with each other every day. Hold on to who *you* are; after all, it's *you* who your man wants to be with! Remember that! My hope is that you do all these things.

Also, remember the things that made you want to be with each other in the first place. Remember that you care about making each other happy. Remember that you enjoy spending time together. Remember that you are interested in knowing what the other person is thinking about. Remember that this is the person whom you want to experience life with. Remember that you love him! And please don't ever forget that you deserve to be loved … it's your right! No one or no thing can take that away from you! My hope is that you remember these things!

Just like life, I think that relationships occur in stages; a beginning, a middle, and an end. While this, in fact, is the end of this book, my hope is that it's just the beginning of the journey that leads you to a lifetime of full, meaningful, and rewarding relationships!

Pop Quiz

1. You and your man have been together for two years now, and things couldn't be better. He's open, honest, and kind. Physically, you couldn't ask for more. Intellectually, you seem to "get" each other. Even your families like each other. And both your lives seem to be moving in the same general direction. You know it sounds corny, but you honestly seem to fall more in love with him every day, as he does with you! One Saturday night during the midst of a weekend getaway, you're climbing into bed after a long day of fun, relaxation, and general revelry. You

pull the covers back and are almost blinded by the shear wattage of what appears to be one singularly spectacular diamond ring (princess cut ... he remembered!). You turn around to ask him what's going on, and there he is, on bended knee! This is the moment, and he pops the question. What do you say?

A. Nothing, you can only cry.
B. Nothing, you can only scream.
C. Nothing, you can only hyperventilate.
D. Yes!

Answer: D. Well, I hope you get to D at some point soon, after going through a little bit of A, B, and C. Sometimes one plus one equals two. Sometimes right is right. Sometimes it's just that simple. Sometimes it's just that obvious ... congratulations!

Afterword

One of the reasons I decided to write this book was because of forgiveness. Women are very understanding, nurturing, and forgiving individuals. It never ceases to amaze me, the good they are usually able to see in men when the rest of the world only sees something less. I tell my friends and patients alike: women will forgive a lot of things you do, but they will not forgive a lie. Once you lie to them, the trust is broken. Once the trust is broken, it is highly unlikely she will ever again be able to give herself to you completely (mind, body, and soul). It is that disconnect that may grow and eventually cause the end of your relationship. See, guys, lying isn't just about us. Lying means that we didn't trust her enough to allow her the opportunity to handle our truth with love, care, and respect and then to say and do what's best for both of us and what she felt was right. It's a hard concept to understand, but trust me, it is huge, and it's a critical skill to master.

The difference in how women and men operate is sometimes astounding. Women feel it in their hearts. Men believe it in their heads. Women talk it out. Men act it out. Women express it. Men repress it. In understanding the basic differences in how women and men behave, we can begin to understand and master effective and honest communication in our relationships.

I know some of you are feeling a little beat up and bruised by the brutality of some of the "pop quizzes." It was a necessary evil. Things aren't always as deceitful and cloak-and-dagger as

I portrayed them to be. But sometimes they are! Sometimes things are sinister. Sometimes things are life-altering. My goal there was not to shock you but to help point out to you how little things can become big issues if you're not paying attention. Most, if not all, of the examples and scenarios I use in this book are purposely overgeneralized to the extreme. This is to clear away any ambiguity about the situation itself, knowing that, in most of our lives, we may only encounter bits and pieces of any one of these given scenarios.

What I hope I've given you here, ladies, are clues and trues. Clues as to how the male mind works (because, Lord knows, we all need all the clues we can get). And I've given you true-to-life experiences or situations that, even though they might not match yours exactly, you may be able to apply some of the same principles to your own situations.

References

1. U.S. Department of Health and Human Services, Centers for Disease Control and Prevention, National Center for Health Statistics (2007). http://www.cdc.gov/nchs/fastats/divorce.htm
2. U.S. Department of Health and Human Services, Centers for Disease Control and Prevention, National Center for Health Statistics (2007). http://www.cdc.gov/nchs/fastats/divorce.htm
3. Sheslow, D. V. (2007). The Nemours Foundation, KidsHealth. http://kidshealth.org/kid/feeling/thought/sadness.html
4. Patten, P. (1999). "Divorce and Children, Part I: An Interview with Robert Hughes, Jr., PhD." Parent News.
5. http://www.athealth.com/consumer/disorders/childrendivorce.html4
6. Merriam-Webster Online Dictionary (2009). www.merriam-webster.com/
7. Cyprah (2008). "9 Tell-Tale Signs of Poor Communication in Relationships." http://mscyprah.newsvine.com/_news/2008/03/15/1368419-9-tell-tale-signs-of-poor-communication-in-relationships-
8. The Centers for Disease Control and Prevention and The National Institute of Justice, (2000). "Extent, Nature, and Consequences of Intimate Partner Violence."

9. Merriam-Webster Online Dictionary (2009). www.merriam-webster.com/

10. Stevens, Ben (2007). "5 Main Reasons of Divorce." South Carolina Family Law Blog http://www.scfamilylaw.com/2008/06/articles/divorce/the-main-reasons-people-divorce/